Are You the One?

Other Titles in the
Teaching Sermon Series

UNMERITED FAVOR
Teaching Sermons on the Love and Grace of God
David Albert Farmer

THE TEACHING SERMON SERIES

Ronald J. Allen, Editor

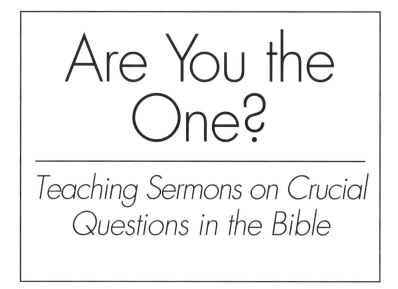

Are You the One?

Teaching Sermons on Crucial Questions in the Bible

WILLIAM D. WATLEY

Abingdon Press
Nashville

Watley, William D.
    Are you the one? : teaching sermons on crucial questions in the Bible / William D. Watley.
      p.   cm.— (The teaching sermon series)
    Includes bibliographical references.
    ISBN 0-687-02614-8 (pbk. : alk. paper)
    1. Teaching sermons. 2. Sermons, American. I. Title.
    II. Series.
    BV4253.W355A74   1997
    252—dc21   97-11788
                                                               CIP

Scripture quotations unless otherwise noted are from the Revised Standard Version of the Bible, copyright 1946, 1952, 1971 by the Division of Christian Education of the National Council of the Churches of Christ in the USA. Used by permission.

Scripture quotations from the *Holy Bible: New International Version* are copyright © 1973, 1978, 1984 by the International Bible Society. Used by permission of Zondervan Bible Publishers.

Scripture quotations from the New Revised Standard Version Bible are copyright © 1989, by the Division of Christian Education of the National Council of the Churches of Christ in the United States of America.

Scripture quotations noted KJV are from the King James Version of the Bible.

97 98 99 00 01 02 03 04 05 06—10 9 8 7 6 5 4 3 2 1

MANUFACTURED IN THE UNITED STATES OF AMERICA

There are a number of people whose assistance made this book a reality. I continue to be grateful to Mrs. Carolyn Scavella, sister and friend, for her insightful and critical assistance. My administrative assistant Connie A. Wilson, along with Ellen Warren and Constance Neal, deciphered my handwritten manuscripts and typed them, since my computer skills are still in their infancy stages. The people of St. James African Methodist Episcopal Church are patient and encouraging listeners, and my wife Muriel is patient with me in my less than stellar moments.

I wish to dedicate this book especially to two persons—one living and one departed. My uncle, Mr. William Day, is the stabilizing force in our extended family who keeps everyone connected. The older I get, the more I love him. I hope this book will add to the joyousness of his spirit.

Also, I hold in sacred memory Miss Louise Warren, a former administrative assistant, ardent church worker, and competent colleague in ministering to the needs of the saints. I celebrate the gift that she was to so many people by dedicating this book also to her.

Contents

Foreword

DYNAMIC TEACHING OF THE CHRISTIAN FAITH BUILDS strong congregations that make a vital witness. Faithful Christian teaching helps the Christian community respond to the two most important questions in life. Who are we in the light of the gospel? What does the gospel call us to do? *The Teaching Sermon Series* aims to provide examples of effective teaching sermons.

The time is ripe for a focus on the teaching ministry of the pulpit. Teaching is a prominent emphasis in the preaching of many congregations that are growing in size, in depth of Christian commitment, and in outreach. Teaching sermons appeal to many people today. Further, many contemporary congregations (particularly in the old-line denominations) are declining because they do not have a distinctive sense of Christian identity and mission or a sufficient flow of spiritual energy. Teaching sermons invite diminished churches to the new life that can come when the resources of the gospel, the Bible, Christian tradition, and doctrine are integrated into everyday Christian experience.

The people of God are by nature a teaching community, as Deuteronomy makes clear: "Hear, O Israel: The LORD is our God, the LORD alone. . . . Recite [these words] to your children and talk about them when you are at home and when you are away, when you lie down and when you rise . . . " (Deut. 6:4-9 NRSV). Teaching is constitutive of the identity of the leaders of the people of God as we recognize by recalling the teaching dimensions of some of the formative ministries of our tradition: Moses, Deborah, Ezra, Jesus, Paul,

Priscilla, Origen, Augustine, Catherine of Siena, Luther, Calvin, Wesley, King, Malcolm, McFague, Dozier, Suchocki. A great cloud of witnesses empowers the pastor who would teach from the pulpit.

Teaching sermons have their best effect when they are part of a systemic approach to teaching Christian faith that permeates the Christian community. In the congregational setting, the sermon can play key roles in helping a community develop a consciousness for learning. First, the sermon can be a significant moment of teaching and learning in its own right. The service of worship is the largest regular gathering of the congregation. In a single moment, the preacher has the opportunity to touch the heart, mind, and will of the community. Second, by modeling the vitalization that results from Christian teaching, the sermon can encourage the members of the congregation to take part in the smaller learning groups that are a part of the congregation's life. Third, the sermon can sensitize the congregation to the ways in which the gospel is taught (or not taught) in all that happens in the life of the church.

As I point out in an earlier book, *The Teaching Sermon* (Nashville: Abingdon Press, 1995), there is no single format for teaching sermons. Teaching and learning can take place in multiple ways. Some educational sermons are linear in sequence and informational in tone, while others are associative and evocative. Many teaching sermons combine sequential and associative approaches. Some teaching sermons center on biblical texts or themes, while others give an interpretation of Christian doctrine, while still others help the congregation reflect on contemporary theological and moral issues. The subjects and methods of Christian teaching are as varied as life itself. *The Teaching Sermon Series* illustrates the variety in both style and content that is possible when the preacher is a teacher.

Ronald J. Allen

Introduction

SEVERAL YEARS AGO A COLLEAGUE, THE REVEREND DR. MAC Charles Jones, pastor of St. Stephens Baptist Church in Kansas City, Missouri, and I were discussing a subject that preachers love to talk about—preaching. During the course of conversation the subject of the questions in the Bible arose. I said that I had been fascinated by them for a long time and had thought about preaching a series of sermons on them. The Reverend Jones indicated that he had just completed a year-long series on the questions of scripture and encouraged me to pursue such a collection of messages. This book is partly the result of that conversation.

The questions that we find in the Scriptures can be very intriguing. Sometimes the questions are those put by God or Christ to humans. Sometimes they are asked by individuals of God or Jesus. Sometimes the questions are answered and sometimes they are not. Many of the questions of the Bible are crucial to life, both here and hereafter.

I have received new insight into many familiar passages of scripture, and others have taken on new meaning, as I focused on the questions. I invite you to journey with me as the Holy Spirit directs, as we examine some of the crucial questions that confront us in Scripture.

William D. Watley
Fall 1996

Chapter One

Is There Any Word from the Lord?

Jeremiah 37:16-17

EVERY WEEK MANY OF US COME to church in the throes of struggle asking the question: "Is there any word from the Lord?" Every day news comes to us across the airwaves about communities, nations, and a whole world in turmoil. Thus we come to church seeking a word of hope and direction in these maddening times. We come asking the age-old question that King Zedekiah put to the prophet Jeremiah, "Is there any word from the LORD?" We come with feelings of desperation and with searching spirits and we say to God's messenger, "I need to hear from heaven. Things around me are changing before my eyes, and I feel sadly out of touch with those persons and institutions that I have given myself to."

"I don't understand my family and my family doesn't seem to understand me. I don't understand my church and my church doesn't seem to understand me. I don't understand what is happening on my job and my job doesn't seem to care about what's happening with me. I don't understand what's happening in school with the subjects or curriculum, with teachers, with some of the administrative policies, and with my peers. And they don't seem to understand me. I don't understand what is happening in my community and neighborhood, and it doesn't understand that I'm beginning to feel like a stranger on my own turf. I don't understand what's happening in the world today, and the world seems to be passing me by. Everywhere I turn I meet others who are just as confused, just as powerless, and with just as many questions as I have. The church is my last and only real hope. Thus I come with this question: "Is there any word from the LORD?"

Our age desperately needs a word from the Lord, yet in our time, so many questions are being raised about the credibility of the institutions, the church, and its representatives—the preachers—who are supposed to provide that word. It seems that every time we turn on the television or pick up the newspaper we see a story about financial mismanagement of some religious institution, or how some believer's life was misdirected because of the erroneous teaching of some religious group, or the personal moral indiscretion of some religious leader. It almost seems as if it's open season on the church. In the midst of all of this, we, as believers, would like to know, "Is there any word from the LORD?"

In a morally complex culture in which we are confronted by abortion, genetic engineering, in vitro fertilization or test-tube babies, surrogate parenting or "wombs for hire," euthanasia or the cutting off of life-support systems, we need to know as we grapple with these sensitive ethical issues, "Is there any word from the LORD?"

Forces of evil and destruction seem out of control. The environment is being decimated. More and more nations are being armed with nuclear weapons. The international drug cartel has infiltrated world economics and politics on a systemic level and ruined so many lives on an individual level that some have begun to talk about legalizing what is, in essence, a slow system of death. The gap between the haves and have-nots is becoming more and more unbridgeable. There is a crucial question we are asking in the midst of all that we see: Is there any word from the Lord?

When King Zedekiah asked this question of the prophet Jeremiah, the Babylonians who had been besieging Jerusalem had withdrawn to contend with the Egyptians whose armies were marching to the defense of the people of Judah. King Zedekiah had begun to hope that Jerusalem might be saved after all. He called for the prophet Jeremiah who had been imprisoned because of his unpopular preaching. Jeremiah had declared that Jerusalem would fall because the judgment of God was upon it and he had counseled the king and citizens of the land to surrender to the Babylonians and plead for mercy. Jeremiah's preaching may have been good prophecy, but it was bad politics. Good religion, devotion to truth, and ultimate allegiance to God do not always make for good politics. If politics is the art of compromise, then sometimes we must choose between our convictions about right and wrong—the morally excellent way—and the way of political expediency.

> *Good religion, devotion to truth, and ultimate allegiance to God do not always make for good politics.*

Moses' deliverance of the nonnegotiable demand to Pharaoh to let God's people go may have been a great act of courage, but it was bad politics. Elijah telling Ahab that rain would be withheld from the land because of Israel's apostasy, and Micaiah's warning him to desist from his desire to capture Ramoth in Gilead may have been good prophecy, but they were examples of bad politics. Nathan's confrontation of David with his sin of adultery and his complicity in the murder of Uriah may have been good prophecy, but it was bad politics. Daniel's praying three times a day in defiance of the king's order and the three Hebrew boys' refusal

to bow before Nebuchadnezzar's golden image may have
been acts of good religion, but they were bad politics.

John the Baptist's public condemnation of the marriage of
Herod and Herodias may have been good prophecy, but it
was bad politics. Jesus' criticism of the scribes and the Phar-
isees may have been good religion, and his cleansing of the
temple may have been good prophecy, but both were bad
politics. Jesus' refusals to cater to Annas or Caiaphas, to
speak to Herod, or to buddy up to Pilate may have been
good prophecy, but they were bad politics. Peter and John's
statement before the Sanhedrin that they must obey God
rather than human beings, may have been good religion but
it was bad politics. The refusal of the early Christians to say
"Caesar is Lord," may have been good religion, but it was
bad politics. Sometimes we must make a decision between
good religion and bad politics, between saying the right
thing or the popular thing.

Jeremiah may not have been a good politician but his
prophecy, his truth, was on target. Consequently when King
Zedekiah, the master politician, wanted to know the truth he
sent for Jeremiah, the bad politician who would deliver the
truth. There are times when we need somebody who will tell
us the truth. There are times when we don't need people
around us without backbone who play games with us, who
will cater to our ego or position, or who will first be concerned about protecting their popularity, office, or turf—
those who will slant the truth to their advantage because
they are pursuing some personal agenda. Who is the person
who loves us the most—that person who will tell us the
truth? Who is our best friend—that person who will tell us
the truth? Who is the most valuable ally in a crisis—that
person who will tell us the truth? Who is our strongest and
most loyal supporter—not the one who tells us what he or
she thinks we want to hear, but that individual who will tell
us the truth—whether it hits us or them? When our fate and

the fate of Jerusalem is in question, when our well-being and the well-being of God's people and God's program are uncertain, when we're wrestling with life-and-death issues, we don't need any mealymouthed sycophants around us. We don't need anybody trying to throw a rock and hide his or her hand. We need somebody who will tell us the truth.

> *Who is the person who loves us the most—that person who will tell us the truth? Who is our best friend—that person who will tell us the truth? Who is the most valuable ally in a crisis—that person who will tell us the truth?*

As Zedekiah wondered about the fate of Jerusalem, whether it would live or fall, whether the Babylonians would return or not, he asked Jeremiah a very crucial question, "Is there any word from the LORD?" If we want the right answer, if we really want to know the truth, we must not only ask the right person, we must ask the right question. Zedekiah asked the right question. He didn't ask, "Is there a word from the prophets association?" Or, "Jeremiah, what is your personal opinion?" He didn't ask, "What are the officials of my kingdom saying?" He didn't ask, "Is there any word from the economist about the value of our currency?" He didn't ask, "What are the rich and powerful saying?" He didn't ask, "Is there any word from the academic or professional community?" He didn't ask, "Is there any word from my generals or political analysts?" He didn't ask, "What are the masses, the people saying?" Zedekiah knew that there was only one source of truth that he could really rely upon, and he identified that source in his question, "Is there any word from the LORD?"

Jeremiah told Zedekiah, "There is a word from the Lord and it's the same word that I have delivered before. You

shall be delivered into the hand of the king of Babylon."
There is consistency in God's word. Jeremiah gave no new
word to Zedekiah, but reminded him of an old word already
given that had not been heeded. Prophets come and go,
rulers rise and fall, kingdoms wax and wane, but God's word
is consistent. It doesn't change according to the fashion, or
adjust itself to the liberalization of human attitudes, or
modernize itself for a computerized age.

God's disdain of sin is consistent. God is not any less
offended by sin than God was in the days of Noah and Lot,
or in the days of Sodom and Gomorrah when people ate and
drank, bought and sold and nothing else, until the flood
waters rose and fire fell from heaven. God is not any less
offended by sin than God was on Good Friday when the sun
refused to shine because God's own beloved Son was repre-
senting sin on the cross. God's commitment to justice is consistent. "Thus says the LORD: 'Let not the wise man glory in
his wisdom, let not the mighty man glory in his might, let
not the rich man glory in his riches; but let him who glories
glory in this, that he understands and knows me, that I am
the LORD who practice steadfast love, justice, and righteousness in the earth; for in these things I delight, says the LORD' "
(Jer. 9:23-24). God is still committed to the establishment of
justice, the liberation of the oppressed, the scattering of the
proud in the imagination of their hearts, putting down the
mighty from their thrones, exalting those of low degree, and
announcing the acceptable year of the Lord.

Is there a word from the Lord for our moral crises? Yes
there is and it's called the Ten Commandments. If God said
something was wrong yesterday, then it's wrong today. Cov-
eting is still wrong; taking the Lord's name in vain is still
wrong; enthroning other gods as the center of our alle-
giances and devotion is still wrong. God's standards for
integrity don't change.

God's affirmation of all life and the whole of life is consistent. There is no such thing as illegitimate life. God affirms life in the womb. The Lord told Jeremiah, "Before I formed you in the womb I knew you, and before you were born I consecrated you" (Jer. 1:5). But God is also concerned about the quality of life after birth. Sometimes people become upset about the rights of the unborn but don't care anything

> *God's affirmation of all life and the whole of life is consistent. There is no such thing as illegitimate life.*

about the rights of those already born. Some of the same people who talk about right to life think nothing about voting down social programs and money for education that improve the quality of life after birth. God however affirms life also after birth. It was to those already born that Jesus as God's Anointed declared, "I came that they may have life, and have it abundantly" (John 10:10). God's affirmation of life is consistent. It begins in the womb, is maintained after birth, and goes beyond death. Paul declared, "For we know that if the earthly tent we live in is destroyed, we have a building from God, a house not made with hands, eternal in the heavens" (2 Cor. 5:1).

But that's not all. When our hearts are heavy and almost breaking in sorrow, there is a word from the Lord that's also needful: "Blessed are those who mourn, for they shall be comforted" (Matt. 5:4). When we're sick and can't get well, there is a word from the Lord: "My grace is sufficient for you, for my power is made perfect in weakness" (2 Cor. 12:9). When we're downcast and discouraged, there is a word from the Lord: "Look at the birds of the air: they neither sow nor reap nor gather into barns, and yet your heavenly Father feeds them. Are you not of more value than they? . . . Consider the lilies of the field, how they grow;

they neither toil nor spin; yet I tell you, even Solomon in all his glory was not arrayed like one of these" (Matt. 6:26, 28-29). When we begin to worry about the church and its program, there is a word from the Lord, "On this rock I will build my church, and the powers of death shall not prevail against it" (Matt. 16:18).

"Is there any word from the LORD?" "There is," said Jeremiah. "You shall be delivered into the hand of the king of Babylon." Zedekiah received a word that would be fulfilled in his own life. The word from the Lord is a living word. God's word is more than a command spoken to chaos that caused worlds to come into being. God's word is more than a written law given on tablets of stone to Moses. God's word is more than a revealed word to prophets and preachers. God's word is a living word. John said: "And the Word became flesh and dwelt among us, full of grace and truth; we have beheld his glory, glory as of the only Son from the Father" (John 1:14).

We have a living Word who walks with us and talks with us, who holds our hands, and answers us when we call. Christmas announces the incarnation of the living Word. Lent is the preparation of the living Word for sacrifice for our redemption. Easter is the victory of the living Word over death and the powers of darkness. "Is there any word from the LORD?" There is!

No wonder one writer said:

> How firm a foundation, ye saints of the Lord,
> Is laid for your faith in his excellent word!
> What more can he say than to you he hath said,
> To you who for refuge to Jesus have fled? . . .
> The soul that on Jesus still leans for repose,
> I will not, I will not desert to its foes;
> That soul, though all hell should endeavor to shake,
> I'll never, no, never, no, never forsake.

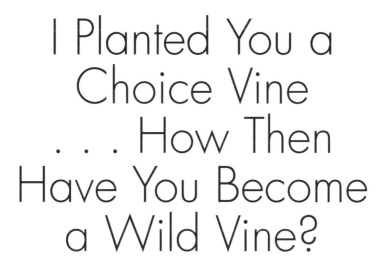

Chapter Two

I Planted You a Choice Vine . . . How Then Have You Become a Wild Vine?

Jeremiah 2:21

JOURNEY WITH ME TO A PRISON WHERE the worst offenders of the law who have committed the most heinous and inhumane crimes are kept. Among society's worst, search out the individuals who are the most vile and repulsive, those who will do or say anything to, or about, anyone without flinching, and without remorse, regret, or repentance. Search out those individuals who have no respect for self, life, morality, or God; whose philosophy is violence and whose creed is survival of the fittest; those who are so mired and enmeshed in wickedness that they are evil to the core. It's hard to imagine that these persons were ever innocent babies with as much potential for good as for evil, and with possibilities for greatness as well as disgrace.

It's hard to imagine an Adolf Hitler, Idi Amin, Charles Manson, or Al Capone, or the drug lords of this era as tiny helpless infants needing their diapers changed, tears wiped away, and having to be held and cuddled as any other baby. The late Bishop E. L. Hickman of the African Methodist Episcopal Church, used to tell young men before he performed their marriage ceremony, "Treat your wife right. Remember the young lady you are about to marry is some father's daughter and some mother's child." Lives that go sour did not appear upon the face of the earth as the disgrace that they have become. They started out innocently as some mother's child and some father's son or daughter. Lest we forget, every criminal, every dreg or waste of humanity, is also the creation of God, planted as a choice and unique vine among us. How then does it become a wild and degenerate vine? What happens to life, to any of us that turns us from a miracle to a mess?

> *Lest we forget, every criminal, every dreg or waste of humanity, is also the creation of God, planted as a choice and unique vine among us.*

What happens in school that turns some students from choice vines into wild vines? What happens in our careers (education, law, medicine, business) to turn some of us from choice vines into wild vines? What happens in church that turns some members from choice vines into wild vines? What happens in the ministry that turns some of us from choice vines into wild vines?

Somebody is asking what happens in my home to turn my children . . . to turn my marriage from a choice vine into a wild vine? How did this relationship that held so much promise go sour? How did this choice vine become a wild vine?

That is the crucial question of this message, and that was the question that Jeremiah, speaking on behalf of God, asked Judah as he looked at what the nation—his own people—had become. At that point in humanity's history, no other nation could claim a heritage like the covenant people of God. No nation could trace their deliverance from slavery and from their enemies to the direct, observable, verifiable, and miraculous intervention of God. No other nation could observe as many miracles in history. What other nation could say that when they were slaves, the water of the land of their bondage became blood, the dust of the earth became lice, ashes became boils upon the bodies of those who enslaved them, and the firstborn of their oppressors were mysteriously slain in one night while death passed over the homes of all slaves whose doorposts were covered with lamb's blood?

What other nation could boast of having a sea open up before them so that they could cross over on dry land and watching as the sea closed upon their pursuing former oppressors? What other nation could boast of being led in the wilderness with manna from heaven in the morning, quail in the evening, and receiving water from the rocks in the driest of places? What other nation could boast that they had received their law not from any parliament or congress, or through any other legislative or political process, but from the fiery finger of God that wrote upon tablets of stone? What other nation could boast of military conquests that came by simply marching around the walls of a great city until it fell down flat? Most nations face the future with a question mark—they hope for a long and powerful life, but their future is uncertain and unknown. God's people were promised a long and productive life if only they followed the law that they had received from God.

Settled in a land that flowed with milk and honey, protected and watched over by the same God whose hand had placed the stars in the midnight sky, Israel had been planted as a choice vine among the nations. The nation, however, that the prophet Jeremiah knew was no longer the apple of heaven's eye, but the object of its judgment. The choice vine had become degenerate and wild. The nation with an eye single to the glory of God had become blind to God's presence and law in its midst. The nation founded on, by, and through faith had become faithless and apostate, reflecting nothing distinctive in either its moral or political life. Jeremiah looked at the great heritage of faith, the noble vision, and the soaring hope for a nation that would be unique in the way it did business. He observed how his own people had strayed from the rock in which they had been hewn and he, speaking for God, asked a crucial question, "Yet I planted you a choice vine, wholly of pure seed. How then have you turned degenerate and become a wild vine?"

When we read Israel's history we observe a number of things that happened that drew it away from its closeness to God—David's own sins that prevented him from exercising proper authority and discipline in his own household; Solomon's apostasy in his old age; the rebellion under Rehoboam and the split of the people of God into the separate kingdoms of Israel and Judah; and a series of rulers whose god was their ambition rather than the Lord. The people of God did not become degenerate overnight, but over time.

Becoming evil or good is a process. We don't suddenly become evil or good. It takes time for both. Sometimes when we decide to lose weight we'll cut back on our eating for a couple of days or weeks, and then become discouraged if we

> **Becoming evil or good is a process. We don't suddenly become evil or good. It takes time for both.**

don't see a dramatic drop in weight. However we can't lose weight in a week when we have spent years putting it on. We cannot shake desires overnight that we've been nurturing for years. We can't stop loving someone overnight that we've been loving for years. If we can stop loving someone overnight, we really didn't love the person to begin with. There is no such phenomenon as love at first sight. There may be mutual attraction, interest, curiosity, and possible desire, at first sight. But it takes time to grow into, and out of, true love. Marriages and relationships do not soar overnight, but over time. We do not build love and lasting relationships overnight but over time. Diets help us lose weight, but only a change of lifestyle helps us to keep off the weight we've lost. And changes in lifestyle take time. Sin is a lifestyle. Resistance to sin is like a diet, but holiness and righteousness that help us to overcome sin are changes of lifestyle that take time. Rome wasn't built in a day, and neither is our character.

The body does not break down overnight but over time. Health and wholeness are not recovered overnight but over time. Skills are not mastered, knowledge is not thoroughly learned, and wisdom and experience are not gained overnight, but over time. We do not become mean and embittered, negative and cynical, selfish and self-centered, greedy and dishonest overnight, but over time. Neither do we develop sweetness and cheerfulness, unselfishness and generosity, positive attitudes and outlook overnight, but over time. We do not lose our souls and our integrity, our perspective and our values overnight, but over time. Neither do we regain a sense of purpose, our self-respect and confidence, our closeness to God overnight, but over time. How does a choice vine become degenerate? Over time.

Over time we stopped praying and reading the Bible regularly. Over time we stopped attending church; we became sloppy in our private devotions, in our preparation; we stopped caring . . . over time.

I planted you a choice vine. . . . Did we allow some disappointments to turn our heads—disappointments regarding our timetables and personal agendas as we see the meteoric rise and success of others? Did we become disappointed with other people?

Did we trust a Judas who betrayed us? A Simon Peter, a best friend who failed us? Did we encounter a hypocritical Ananias or Sapphira, a doubting Thomas or a James and John who are always working on their own agendas? What about the fickled masses who shout "Hosanna" one day and crucify the next?

Have we been disappointed with God? We forget that God has a right to be disappointed with us. Yet in spite of God's disappointment with us, God keeps on blessing us, answering prayer, getting us out of messes. Then, once we were disappointed, we started listening to the devil. The devil is a master at playing on our disappointment.

> *Have we been disappointed with God? We forget that God has a right to be disappointed with us.*

However, there is a word of hope for us and others and it is this: No matter how far we have fallen, how much we have failed and erred, we can be redeemed. Jeremiah learned that lesson one day when he went down to the potter's house. There he saw the potter working with a lump of clay trying to shape it into a vessel. However, the vessel that the potter made was spoiled. What did the potter do? Did he throw away the clay? Did he give up trying to be a potter? No, he worked the clay into another vessel.

Sometimes choice vines become wild. But God does not give up on the vine; neither does God cease being a good God because a choice vine has become wild. Instead God performs a divine grafting procedure. When two plants are grafted, they are cut so that their living cells are exposed; they are then joined together so that they grow into each other and become one. Two plants cannot be grafted together, however, unless both are wounded. On Calvary, Jesus was wounded for our sins and bruised for our iniquities. When he was speared in the side, blood of redemption and waters of cleansing baptism flowed. When we bring our

> *Sometimes choice vines become wild. But God does not give up on the vine; neither does God cease being a good God because a choice vine has become wild.*

wounded lives, our broken hearts and contrite spirits, our confession of need, our desire and determination to do better to Jesus, we become grafted to Jesus and he to us, and the wildness in our character is replaced by his peace.

Choice vines turned wild can become choice vines again. Across the ages I hear the voice of Jesus saying:

"I am the true vine, and my Father is the vinedresser. . . . Abide in me, and I in you. As the branch cannot bear fruit by itself, unless it abides in the vine, neither can you, unless you abide in me. I am the vine, you are the branches." (John 15:1, 4-5)

Chapter Three

Where Is the Word of the Lord?

| Jeremiah 17:15 |

THIS CRUCIAL QUESTION IS ONE THAT comes from the prophecy of Jeremiah. I have always admired the prophet Jeremiah for his willingness, and even daring, to ask God questions, some of which are the same that perplex my own faith. In Jeremiah we find the turmoil of a real saint struggling to be faithful to his calling and to the word of the Lord. At times Jeremiah was lonely because he told the truth as he saw it, and truth is not always popular. At times Jeremiah was depressed because the truth that he spoke was against his own people, and unlike so many of us, Jeremiah took no delight in being a bearer of bad news. At times Jeremiah was frustrated because God's word and will seemed to move at a snail's pace toward fulfillment, or they appeared to stand still, making themselves null and void.

One of the factors that few of us take into account when we pray and ask God to do certain things or when we receive a revelation or message from the Lord is how long it takes for that vision, request, or word to be fulfilled. Since something is from the Lord and since we know God has all power and can answer us even before we call, we expect God to move *right now* and there are times when God does act instantly. However, there are other times when, like a seed growing secretly, God works through, and in, the ordinary, slow moving processes of nature and of history.

> One of the factors that few of us take into account when we pray and ask God to do certain things or when we receive a revelation or message from the Lord is how long it takes for that vision, request, or word to be fulfilled.

Birth is the handiwork of God, for only God can create or make life. (Thus only God has the right to take life.) God who is powerful enough to create and maintain all life in the universe is also able to create life instantaneously. However, no births have ever been recorded as having come forth in the twinkling of an eye, without having gone through the normal process of development and growth in the womb. Even Jesus, God's only begotten son, was not born the very instant that the angel revealed to Mary that she would have a child. Even though the child within her was uniquely the work of the Holy Spirit, Mary's pregnancy was still full term. She and Joseph had to wait until the fullness of time before the child that was revealed and prophesied was born. So it is with the word of the Lord, and answers to prayers, in our lives. There is often a large span of time between the moment of revelation and the moment of consummation.

Noah received the revelation that God was going to cleanse the earth by water and that he was to build an ark. However, he had to preach, prepare, and build a long time before the first rain cloud appeared in the sky and before the first raindrop fell from heaven. All the while he had to hear the daily jeering and jesting of an unbelieving world that mocked the old man for building a boat in the middle of the desert.

When they were far beyond their childbearing years, Abraham and Sarah were told that they would have a son. However, in spite of their advanced years, Isaac was still not born until twenty-five years later. All the while Abraham and Sarah were wandering nomads in search of a place to call home.

When he was a mere teenager, David was told that he would be Israel's next king. However, many years passed between the moment that Samuel anointed him in his father's house, and when he was actually crowned in Hebron. During that time he was hunted like an outlaw, and treated as an outcast in his own land.

At the beginning of his ministry, Jeremiah received the message that because Judah had long forsaken God, it would fall to the hand of Babylon. God did not hastily pronounce judgment upon Judah. God had labored too long in establishing these people to hastily bring judgment upon them. God reminded them in Exodus, "You have seen what I did to the Egyptians, and how I bore you on eagles' wings and brought you to myself" (19:4). The people of God had long abandoned their faith tradition, a whole series of apostate kings had come to the throne, and a number of prophets—known and unknown—had arisen to warn Judah of her sins before God declared "enough is enough."

How blessed all of us are that God's word of judgment is not hastily given or fulfilled, for if it were, a number of us presently sitting here would not be here. We as humans —especially we Christians—tend to send people to hell much quicker than God does. The atheist Robert Ingersoll, after finishing a lecture, took out his watch and declared to his audience, "I will . . . give [God] five minutes to strike me dead [for the things I have said]." The minutes slowly ticked off as he held his watch and waited. After the audience waited for what seemed an eternity, Ingersoll decisively put his watch in his pocket, seemingly proving that God doesn't exist. When the Reverend Joseph Parker heard about the incident he said, "And did the American gentleman think he could exhaust the patience of God in five minutes?"

We as humans—especially we Christians—tend to send people to hell much quicker than God does.

When we think about how far and how often we fall short of the glory of God, we should realize how blessed we are that God is patient with our foolishness. However, lest we believe that justice delayed means that it is nonexistent or that we can presume on God's mercy, the psalmist reminds us that while "the LORD is merciful and gracious, slow to anger and abounding in steadfast love. He will not always chide, nor will he keep his anger for ever" (103:8-9). When judgment comes, it comes as a result of our having refused, time after time, to repent, obey, or heed God's word.

Jeremiah didn't have God's patience or God's eternity, therefore he grew anxious for God's word to be fulfilled. Jeremiah was not delighted at the thought of his people suffering for their sins. He was called the weeping prophet because he was grieved by the wrongdoing of his people and pained because of the message of judgment that he brought. Jeremiah anxiously awaited the vindication of the prophetic word that he had delivered for so long. Jeremiah began his ministry, according to some estimates, around 627 B.C.E. Jerusalem did not fall to the Babylonians until 588–87 B.C.E. Thus for forty years, Jeremiah would preach a consistent message about the coming of God's judgment upon Jerusalem. Forty years is a long time to believe and declare anything without seeing it fulfilled. Forty years is a long time to predict that something is going to happen without seeing it happen. Forty years is a long time to stand by yourself, being persecuted at times, mocked at times, misunderstood at times, and totally disregarded at times. Forty years is a long time to proclaim an unpopular prophecy or state an unpopular message in the face of overwhelming opposition.

Jeremiah may be a hero to us, but he was no hero while he lived. His message was regarded as treasonous by the political rulers. The religious leadership looked upon him as an outcast. His family was embarrassed by him, and the masses considered him to be a crackpot. Let us remember that greatness and truth often go unrecognized in their own time. Malcolm X has a larger following in death than he did in life. Martin Luther King, Jr.'s true prophetic stature is recognized more easily now than when he lived. When he lived, King was branded a communist by White conservatives and an Uncle Tom by Black militants. When he lived, he was pelted with stones by angry Whites in Chicago and pelted with eggs by angry Blacks in Harlem. When he died, King was under pressure from Blacks and Whites, from the Civil Rights leadership as well as establishment

> *Let us remember that greatness and truth often go unrecognized in their own time.*

politicians because of his stand against the Vietnam War—which was the minority and unpopular position at the time—and his proposed Poor Peoples march.

Lest we forget, Jesus had a much larger following in death than in life. Historians of that era do not regard his life, works, ministry, or death, or those whom he directly touched as having any major significance. His crucifixion was not a major international or national event, but was local news.

No, Jeremiah, like many before and after him who stand in the tradition of prophetic truth, was not popular in his

where is the word of the Lord.
when ... ?

day, and his message was not well received. While he lived, the more acceptable message proclaimed and affirmed by the majority was that Jerusalem would not fall but would be saved. They told Jeremiah, "You've been preaching your gloom-and-doom sermons and depressing people for years. You're been declaring 'Thus saith the Lord' for years. Well, our message has been confirmed. Despite what you have been preaching, Jerusalem is still standing. Where is the validation of the work of the Lord that you've been proclaiming? Let it come."

Where is the word of the Lord? That's the question we ask sometimes when the time is long between promises and fulfillment. Where is the word of the Lord? That's the question we ask when the workers of iniquity and the foes of righteousness seem to have the upper hand. Where is the word of the Lord? That's the question when we feel overwhelmed by opposition and obstacles and doubt begins to eat away at our conviction. Where is the word of the Lord? That's the question when it seems our prayers are not being answered and our trying to live right seems to be for naught. Where is the word of the Lord? That's the question we ask when we see the wicked prospering and scoundrels enjoying peace and justice being denied, while the good suffer.

Where is the word of the Lord? Jeremiah received no answer to this question. There had been other times when Jeremiah had questioned God and the Lord had spoken to him. However, the prophet received no answer this time. Perhaps the message for Jeremiah and for us is that sometimes we have to wait for an answer to the question. Where is the word of the Lord? If we have been faithful and have done all we know to do and have done our best, if we have obeyed what we believe to be the word of the Lord, sometimes we just have to wait in faith for that word to come to pass. It is not ours to know the times or the seasons of God's word, but it is ours to believe God's word and to trust God to keep God's word.

Where is the word of the Lord? Just wait, we'll find out. David said, "I have seen a wicked man overbearing, and towering like a cedar of Lebanon. Again I passed by, and lo,

> *It is not ours to know the times or the seasons of God's word, but it is ours to believe God's word and to trust God to keep God's word.*

he was no more; though I sought him, he could not be found" (Ps. 37:35-36). Where is the word of the Lord? Just wait, we'll find out. "Do not be deceived; God is not mocked, for whatever a man sows, that he will also reap" (Gal. 6:7). Where is the word of the Lord? Just wait, we'll find out. "For still the vision awaits its time; it hastens to the end—it will not lie. If it seem slow, wait for it; it will surely come, it will not delay. Behold, he whose soul is not upright in him shall fail, but the righteous shall live by his faith" (Hab. 2:3-4). Where is the word of the Lord? Just wait, we'll find out. "The grass withers, the flower fades; but the word of our God will stand for ever" (Isa. 40:8).

Where is the word of the Lord? Just wait, we'll find out. John declared on Patmos, "Then I saw heaven opened, and behold, a white horse! He who sat upon it is called Faithful and True, and in righteousness he judges and makes war. His eyes are like a flame of fire, and on his head are many [crowns] . . . and the name by which he is called is The Word of God" (Rev. 19:11-13).

Where do we get faith to wait? We can wait because even though there is no answer in the present, we have an experience in our past of God who always keeps his word. Therefore, if our loved ones have gone astray and we've done all and con-

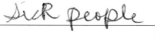

tinue to do all we can, just wait for our effectual fervent prayers to work through time; our loved ones will come to themselves and turn their wandering feet back home. If evil is prospering after we've taken our stand for truth and right, just wait. The battle for righteousness is not ours, but the Lord's. If sick persons whom we love don't seem to get well, if we have put them in the hands of the Lord, all we can do is wait for God who does all things well to deliver either in time or in eternity. If life for us has gone on hold and we have done everything we can to get it back on track, sometimes all we can do is wait for our change to come. And change it will, for weeping may endure for a night but joy does come in the morning.

We can wait because we know that God is still in charge. It is said that one morning a great evangelist came down for breakfast depressed and miserable. His devout wife looked at him, went upstairs, put on a black dress, and came down to join him. The evangelist looked at her and asked, "Who is dead?" "God," she replied. "No, God isn't," the evangelist said. "I thought he was," the wife retorted, "by the way you're looking and the way you're acting." Sometimes, like Jeremiah, we become a little anxious and weary in our waiting, and sometimes, like the evangelist, we get a little discouraged and depressed; but remember, God still lives and watches over God's own.

Another pastor once awoke in the night depressed and worried over a problem. He tossed and turned until about four o'clock in the morning when he decided to really put the matter in God's hand. He felt peace come over him and heard a voice speak to him that said, "This is God. You may go to sleep now. I am awake."

Every now and then, when, like Jeremiah, we become anxious about when the Lord is going to move, God's word and spirit reminds us that the Lord is awake and still in charge. Where is the word of the Lord? It's in the hand of a God who is awake.

Chapter Four

Hast Thou Utterly Rejected Us?

| Lamentations 5:19-22 |

THIS CRITICAL QUESTION IS THE concluding verse of the book of Lamentations. When I read this verse according to the wording of the Revised Standard Version of the Scriptures, I am struck by the fact that the book of Lamentations ends with an unanswered question. This is quite an unusual way to end a biblical book. The only other books that end with a question are Jonah and Nahum. The questions that end these books however are asked of human beings by God. The book of Lamentations however ends with human beings questioning God.

As we are discovering with this series, the Bible abounds with questions, a number of which are those of faithful believers regarding the mysterious ways and workings of God. One of the encouraging aspects of these questions is that in them we see the biblical heroes and heroines wrestling with the same kind of faith questions that perplex us. However, the questions raised in one part of a biblical book are generally answered before the book concludes. The book of Job, for example, is replete with questions. While we admire Job for his patient endurance, we would be mistaken to assume that Job persevered through his trials without asking "Why?" Before the book ended, God answered Job's incessant "Why?" with a series of "Were you there?" questions. When Job questioned God's ways, God showed the superiority of God's ways and wisdom by asking, "Where were you when I laid the foundation of the earth?" Job's faithful, though questioning endurance was justified since all that he lost was restored in greater abundance.

The book of Habakkuk begins with questions. The prophet asks, "O LORD, how long shall I cry for help, and thou wilt not hear? Or cry to thee "Violence!" and thou wilt not save? Why dost thou make me see wrongs and look upon trouble?" (1:2-3). However before the book ends, Habakkuk affirms his faith in God by declaring, "Though the fig tree do not blossom, nor fruit be on the vines, the produce of the olive fail and the fields yield no food, the flock be cut off from the fold and there be no herd in the stalls, yet I will rejoice in the LORD, I will joy in the God of my salvation. GOD, the Lord, is my strength; he makes my feet like hinds' feet, he makes me tread upon my high places" (Hab. 3:17-19).

In 2 Corinthians, Paul raises a question of faith that reflects anxiety. He asks, "Who is sufficient for these things?" In the third chapter, Paul gave the answer when he wrote, "Our sufficiency is of God" (v. 5 KJV). However, because the question raised in Lamentations 5:22 is the concluding verse of the book, there is no answer given to the question that the writer asked God, "Hast thou utterly rejected us? Art thou exceedingly angry with us?"

Biblical scholars, to be sure, have not been comfortable with this ending. Verse 21 reads "Restore us to thyself, O LORD, that we may be restored! Renew our days as of old!" Consequently Jewish rabbis insisted that this verse be read after verse 22 so that the book would end on the more positive and hopeful appeal to God to renew God's people. *The Living Bible* paraphrase also states this verse in the form of a question. A number of other translations, however, have taken the question out of the verse. The King James Version states "But thou hast utterly rejected us; thou art very wroth against us." The New

International Version and the New Revised Standard Version
state, "unless you have utterly rejected us and are angry with us
beyond measure." However, even when the question mark is
taken out of the translation, the question regarding the length
and extent of God's judgment and wrath remains.

One might expect such an ending to a book titled
"Lamentations." To lament is to feel, show, or express grief,
sorrow, or regret. It is to mourn deeply. Composed after the
fall of Jerusalem to the Babylonians, the book of Lamentations is poems, or songs of sorrow, that came from the heart-
break of a people whose world has fallen apart and who are
struggling to maintain some semblance of faith and sanity of
mind. Such African American spirituals as "Nobody Knows
the Trouble I See" and "Sometimes I Feel Like a Motherless
Chile," are expressions of lament. Yet we would be mistaken
if we were to conclude that Lamentations is all sorrow and
no joy, all darkness and no light. One of the Old Testament's
most beautiful expressions of faith comes to us from Lamentations. In the third chapter, we read, "The steadfast love of
the LORD never ceases, his mercies never come to an end;
they are new every morning; great is thy faithfulness. 'The
LORD is my portion,' says my soul, 'therefore I will hope in
him.' The LORD is good to those who wait for him, to the
soul that seeks him. It is good that one should wait quietly
for the salvation of the LORD" (3:22-26).

As the book concludes, the hope and faith of the writer is
still evident. In the final chapter, verse 19 reads, "But thou, O
LORD, dost reign for ever; thy throne endures to all generations." However in verse 20, he asks, "Why dost thou forget
us for ever, why dost thou so long forsake us?" In verse 21, he
prays, "Restore us to thyself, O LORD, that we may be
restored! Renew our days as of old!" In verse 22, he concludes
with the questions, "Or hast thou utterly rejected us? Art thou
exceedingly angry with us?" To understand the authors jock-
eying back and forth between faith and doubt, affirmation and

questions, we must know something about the pain that he felt when Jerusalem fell. I have been reading and preaching about the fall of Jerusalem to the Babylonians for a long time. However, it was not until I read this chapter that I began to really grasp how devastating, mind-blowing, and faith shattering that experience was for the people of God.

Listen to how the writer of Lamentations poured out his heart in this last chapter: "Remember, O LORD, what has befallen us; behold, and see our disgrace! Our inheritance has been turned over to strangers, our homes to aliens. We have become orphans, fatherless; our mothers are like widows. We must pay for the water we drink, the wood we get must be bought. With a yoke on our necks we are hard driven; we are weary, we are given no rest. . . . Slaves rule over us; there is none to deliver us from their hand. We get our bread at the peril of our lives, because of the sword in the wilderness. Our skin is hot as an oven with the burning heat of famine. Women are ravished in Zion, virgins in the towns of Judah. Princes are hung up by their hands; no respect is shown to the elders. Young men are compelled to grind at the mill; and boys stagger under loads of wood. The old men have quit the city gate, the young men their music. The joy of our hearts has ceased; our dancing has been turned to mourning" (5:1-5; 8-15).

When trouble and sickness come and drag on and on; when days turn into weeks, weeks into months, and sometimes months into years, we should try as we might not to doubt or question God, there are times when we can't help feeling for-

> *When trouble and sickness come and drag on and on; when days turn into weeks, weeks into months, and sometimes months into years, we should try as we might not to doubt or question God, there are times when we can't help feeling forsaken.*

saken. One day I was walking down the street of Portland, Oregon, on my way to the unemployment office and it was raining. The rain falling from the sky splashing on my face mixed with tears that were trickling out of my eyes. It had been five months since I had drawn a paycheck. Spring had turned into summer, summer into fall, and winter was approaching. I knew a number of significant personalities in my field and some of them were really trying hard to deliver me, but no one seemed to have been able to do anything. Nothing was opening up in either the field of higher education or the church.

The period of unemployment had lasted much longer than I thought it would, and no end seemed anywhere in sight. In desperation I had even applied for jobs far below my training and couldn't even get them. As I walked down the street that day in the rain I lifted my head to an overcast sky and said, "God, what am I doing here walking down the street in the rain without a job? Why have you allowed my enemies to ruin my career and bring it to a screeching halt? God, will this period ever pass? Will I ever be settled again? Will I ever sit under my own vine and fig tree and have control of my life again?" I understand how the writer of Lamentations must have felt when he asked today's crucial question, "Or hast thou utterly rejected us?"

People who are sick and can neither get well nor die, who, if they have presence of mind must constantly battle anger and self-pity, who have prayed and prayed while heaven has seemed to turn a deaf ear, can't help at times asking this crucial question, "Hast thou utterly rejected us? Art thou exceedingly angry with us?" Persons who have had to live under the stress and in the strain of having a loved one with a lingering illness, who has brought that person before the Lord in earnest prayer and nothing has happened, can't help asking at times, "Hast thou utterly rejected us? Art thou exceedingly angry with us?"

Persons who wonder if their troubles represent God's judgment upon their sins, or if their difficulties are due to their own failings and disobedience, sometimes ask within their spirits even as they plead for mercy, relief, and deliverance, "Hast thou utterly forsaken us? Art thou exceedingly angry with us?" All believing souls, when we feel burdened and depressed, alone and afraid, outnumbered, overhelmed and defeated, falsely accused and misunderstood, find ourselves asking this crucial question, "Hast thou utterly rejected us? Art thou exceedingly angry with us?"

The book of Lamentations ends with this writer's probing inquiry. Unlike Noah, the writer of Lamentations saw no rainbows in the skies to remind him of God's promise. Unlike Jacob, no midnight visitor came to wrestle with him and bless him. Unlike Moses, no burning bush was set afire by heaven to consecrate the ground upon which he stood as holy. Unlike Joshua, no captain of the Lord's host appears to assure him of victory. Unlike Balaam, no dumb animal opens up its mouth to give him a message from heaven. Unlike Gideon, no concrete, visible sign or demonstration is laid before him. Unlike Elijah, no fiery chariots rush to receive him. Unlike Isaiah, he saw no vision in the temple of the glory of God. Unlike Habakkuk, he didn't have the privilege of retreating to a prayer tower and being told that the vision was yet for an appointed time. Unlike Job, no voice came to him out of a whirlwind. Unlike the three Hebrew boys, no visible presence could be seen walking with him in his hour of testing. Unlike Samuel, he heard no one calling him by name.

With the city of Jerusalem sacked, the temple in ruins, the priesthood scattered, and the promised land in foreign hands, all the writer had left was his faith in God and his questions. For although the writer questioned God, he never stopped believing in God. He questioned the extent of God's anger and how far the long arm of divine forgiveness would reach. But he never questioned whether or not God lived. The writer of Lamentations teaches us that sometimes faith must go on living without signs, without systems of support, without voices and visions, and without props. For, the essence of faith is that it dares to stake everything—everything we are, everything we have, everything we believe, everything we hope, everything we dream—on this one central principle: God lives. It is daring to say like Job, "Though he slay me, yet will I trust him" (Job 13:15 KJV).

> *The writer of Lamentations teaches us that sometimes faith must go on living without signs, without systems of support, without voices and visions, and without props.*

"Hast thou utterly rejected us? Art thou exceedingly angry with us?" Although the writer did not record any answer to this question, he still believed. This book teaches us that sometimes having faith means living with unanswered questions. Being a believer doesn't mean that we will be able to explain all that happens. Sometimes we do more harm trying to explain what we don't understand. Crediting everything that happens, everything that mystifies us, to God's will is not the way to do it. Sometimes we have to admit that there are some things we don't understand and some questions we can't answer. Faith is not faith when we have all the answers. Faith is faith when we don't have answers and still believe. The unanswered and the unknown are what make faith faith. If we have all the answers, what we have is not faith, but sight.

> *Being a believer doesn't mean that we will be able to explain all that happens. Sometimes we do more harm trying to explain what we don't understand.*

Faith means saying, "There is much I don't know and can't answer, but one thing I know is that God lives. I don't know why this child was born deformed, or why that person is ill, or why that person died. But this I know: God lives, and because God lives there is meaning and purpose to life. I don't know why this trial or test, problem or trouble has come into my life, but this I know: God lives, and because God lives I know that my life and destiny are not in the hands of aliens—harmful or demonic forces. I don't know how I'm going to make it through this day, this week, this month, or the rest of the year. But this I know: God lives, and because God lives I can face tomorrow. I don't know why certain groups are oppressed, but I know that God lives and so justice will come and evil will be defeated.

"Hast thou utterly rejected us? Art thou exceedingly angry with us?" We know the answer to this question even when we ask it, even as the writer of the book of Lamentations must have known the answer, down in his spirit. If we know anything about God's word, about God's promises, then we know the answer to the question. If we know anything about God's track record and his dealing with his people, we know the answer to the question. If we have had any personal experience with God's deliverance and forgiveness, we know the answer to the question. If we know anything at all about Jesus' sacrifice on Calvary, we know the answer to the question. God never utterly rejects anyone on this side of death. God's anger never exceeds God's forgiveness and restoration.

The Hebrew word *hesed* is often used in the Old Testament. *Hesed* refers to the steadfast love of God. God's stead-

> *God never utterly rejects anyone on this side of death. God's anger never exceeds God's forgiveness and restoration.*

fastness is one of God's most important attributes. God's power doesn't rise and fall with any changing political tide—it's steadfast. God's love is not only plentiful, it's steadfast. God's mercy and truth are steadfast and endure to all generations. God cannot forsake us anymore than the sun can lose its heat and still remain the sun, anymore than the stars can lose their light and still remain stars, anymore than water can lose its wetness and still remain water, anymore than the earth can lose its atmosphere and still remain the earth.

One writer who was looking toward the end of life's journey discovered the answer. He knew that at the end, all we would have to cling to would be the steadfast love of the God who would never leave us, even in a dying hour. Thus he wrote:

> Abide with me; fast falls the eventide;
> The darkness deepens; Lord, with me abide.
> When other helpers fail and comforts flee,
> Help of the helpless, O abide with me.
> Swift to its close ebbs out life's little day;
> Earth's joys grow dim; its glories pass away;
> Change and decay in all around I see;
> O Thou who changest not, abide with me.

Chapter Five

Who Touched Me?

Mark 5:30-31

THIS CRUCIAL QUESTION IS THE response of Jesus to someone who had rubbed him the right way. The question seemed strange to a number of those who heard it because when he asked it, Jesus was in the midst of a crowd. He was on his way to the home of Jairus, a local synagogue administrator, to minister to the daughter of this distressed father. A crowd was following Jesus and people within crowds, because of a crowd's very nature, intrude upon our space, bump into us, and rub shoulders with us. That's why it's important that we are careful about the crowds we travel with.

Never believe that we can travel with the wrong crowd and not be touched by it. It is entirely correct to say, "Bad company ruins good manners." Even the strongest saint can be adversely affected by the wrong crowd. It's hard to hang around consistently with a crowd of drinkers, cursers, smok-

> *Even the strongest saint can be adversely affected by the wrong crowd.*

ers, drug addicts, gossipers, pessimists, and unbelievers and not be influenced by the standards of these crowds.

Many a parent has said to me, "My child isn't bad, he just fell in with the wrong crowd." In the Scriptures, if Rehoboam, the son of Solomon and his successor to the throne, had not listened to the wrong crowd, then he would not have made the wrong administrative decision that resulted in the split of the kingdom of Israel into the northern part known as Israel, and the southern part known as Judah. If the prodigal son had associated with a different crowd, he might not have ended up in a hog pen. Peter did what he considered to be the unbelievable: He denied knowing Jesus. When our Lord was on trial, Peter was hanging out with the wrong crowd.

The crowd we travel with can make a difference in our lives. One of the principles of self-help groups such as Alcoholics Anonymous, Narcotics Anonymous, Sexaholics Anonymous, Overeaters Anonymous, and Gamblers Anonymous is that the crowd we associate with can make a difference in our lives. If the crowd we associate with is supportive of our efforts to do the right thing, then that support can be our salvation. That's what the fellowship of the church is at its best—a support crowd for those who are trying to do the right thing. We're not a perfect crowd, neither are we called to be a judgmental and condemning crowd of those who have made mistakes or who have weaknesses. We're not called to be a negative or faultfinding crowd, or a self-righteous or mean-spirited or arrogant or an elitist crowd—but a support crowd for those who are trying to do the right thing.

If the crowd we associate with is supportive of our wrongdoing, then that crowd can be detrimental to our souls. Sometimes we hold onto certain crowds because we consider them to be our friends. I'm not telling anyone to get rid of his or her friends if they are really friends, but sometimes we need to take a long, hard look at those we consider to be our friends. What are our so-called friends about and what are our so-called friendships about?

My son Matthew and I were driving down the street one night and we saw two teenage boys walking together. Matthew said to me, "I know them. They go to my school and both of them are losers." I told him something that I used to hear older people say when I was young, that I didn't quite understand at the time. I said, "Son, water has a way of seeking its own level." Losers hang out with losers. Drunks hang out with drunks. Cokeheads keep company with cokeheads. Gossipers talk to gossipers. Those with little minds befriend one another.

Sometimes in life we have to choose between our so-called friends and our souls, between our so-called friends and our families, between our so-called friends and those who love us the most. True friends encourage us to do the right thing and if a crowd is not supportive of our efforts to get clean and stay clean; to get sober and stay sober; to get an education, expand our knowledge, or improve ourselves, then the persons in the crowd, no matter what we've done with them in the past or how long we've known them, are not our friends. True friends want what is best for us. Even if they choose to remain behind, true friends will encourage us to do what is best for us.

If you don't remember anything else, remember this: Take heed of the crowd that you associate with. Young man, young woman; married woman, married man; single man and single woman, you may get lonely and discouraged sometimes, but still take heed of the crowd that you associate with.

Jesus was in the midst of a crowd that was rubbing up against him, bumping him, and touching him, when all of a sudden he stopped and asked, "Who touched my garments?" Those physically closest to him were baffled by this question and said, "You see the crowd pressing around you, and yet you say, 'Who touched me?' " Unknown to any of those around him, a woman who had been hemorrhaging for twelve years and who had spent all she had trying to find a cure, to no avail, had come up behind Jesus in the crowd and had touched the fringe of his garments. She had said to herself, "If I touch even his garments, I shall be made well." One would think that such a faith comes by seeing the works of Jesus or hearing the promises of his words for oneself. However, according to the Scriptures, this woman had heard reports about Jesus. There is the possibility that she had never seen Jesus heal anyone. However, she was prepared to *believe* based upon what she had heard. She was prepared to *try* Jesus based upon what she had heard. We do not know how she received the reports concerning Jesus. However, somebody had to bring to her the good news about Jesus' mighty power.

We must never underestimate our importance as individual believers in spreading the gospel. The faith is carried not simply by spellbinding preachers and traveling evangelists, but by individual believers who are unashamed and enthusiastic about sharing the good news of their salvation. How do we win souls for Christ? Simply by telling people what Jesus means to us. We do not win souls by debating or arguing them into the kingdom. We do not win souls by badgering and worrying them into the kingdom. We do not win souls by trying to answer questions about God, the Bible, or our religion that we don't understand ourselves.

> **We must never underestimate our importance as individual believers in spreading the gospel.**

We don't win souls with fake piety and superholiness and religiosity. We don't even win souls by bragging about our church, the preacher, or the choirs.

We win souls to Christ by telling others in language that is plain and simple about what Jesus means to us. As a preacher whose vocation, as well as highest joy, is to help bring souls into the kingdom, I've discovered that I'm most effective not when I tell people about what Jesus did for Paul and Peter, but when I let them know what he's done for me and what he means to me. When I talk about what Jesus has done for others, I am relating what's in my head, and what my mind believes. But when I talk about what Jesus means to me, I am relating what's in my heart, what my life really knows, and what my own experiences can testify to.

What I've said about myself is true for every other believer. If you want to win someone to Christ, tell the person what's in your heart. Tell about what Jesus means to you personally. Your words don't have to be big, your vocabulary impressive, or your knowledge of the Bible that great. But, if what you say truly comes from your heart, then people can tell it and can feel it. *How* you say what you believe, sometimes more than *what* you say about what you believe, is what inspires someone to try Jesus. There will always be persons who know more scripture and can quote it better than you. There will always be persons who can outdebate and outargue you. But nobody, nobody, will know more than you about what the Lord has done for you.

The woman in our text had suffered a long time, and not only had she not gotten any better, but according to Mark, she had gotten worse. Do you know how discouraging it can be to labor with a problem and not only does the situation fail to get better, but things go from bad to worse? It is very frustrating to pray over children and watch as their problems seem to go from bad to worse. It is vexing to try to work out the problems of a relationship and things go from bad to worse. It is

But nobody, nobody, will know more than you about what the Lord has done for you.

depressing to go from doctor to doctor, spend dollar after dollar, take prescription after prescription, try treatment after treatment, and our health goes from bad to worse.

Who is to say that after suffering for twelve years this woman was not ready to give up? Yet at that very moment she either overheard somebody talking or someone told her about a healing prophet from Galilee. That news so rekindled her hope that she dared to venture into a crowd and risk rebuff to seek Jesus. She had no certainty how Jesus would respond to her, but based upon what she had heard, she dared to believe.

Who is to say, your testimony may be the very thing that the persons to whom you are speaking need to hear at that very moment. They may be so discouraged in spirit that they may be at their breaking points. They may be considering suicide or on the verge of mental breakdowns. They may be ready to take another drink or be ready for a quick fix. They may be just plain ready to give up. Perhaps what they need to hear at that point in their lives is your testimony that, "When I was sick, God's power healed me. When I was down, God's love lifted me. When I was lost, God's mercy found me. When I was bound, the power of Jesus' redeeming love freed me. When I didn't know how I was going to make it, the Lord stepped in and made a way out of no way." Your words, not the preacher's or somebody else's that you consider better equipped than you, *your words* may be what these distressed and embattled souls need to hear, that will motivate them to search out Jesus for themselves and reach for him with such power that he pauses to ask, "Who touched me?"

What was there in this woman's touch that caused Jesus to pause? What does it mean to rub Jesus the right way? First, hers was a crowd-defying and determined touch. Her condition meant that she was ceremonially unclean and as such, even the temple was off-limits to her. She was shut off from the place that could give her the hope that she needed. Illness is bad enough, but when there is a stigma attached to it, one has a double cross to bear. Troubles plus isolation and loneliness are a doubly bitter pill to swallow. When those we would expect to support us pull away from us and shun us, the pain of our affliction cuts like a double-edged sword. Any burden is especially torturous when we have to bear it by ourselves, when people are ashamed or afraid to admit that they know us.

> *Troubles plus isolation and loneliness are a doubly bitter pill to swallow.*

Sometimes, as the people of God, our attitudes shut others off from the house of God. Our attitudes about certain kinds of illnesses, certain kinds of trouble, certain weaknesses (forgetting that all have sinned and fallen short of the glory of God), our attitudes about how people look or dress, or how they talk, our attitudes about people's backgrounds or their past mistakes, can make them feel shut off and isolated from the very place they can receive help. If we—who have clothing and shelter, food and family, job and education, looks and health—still need to hear a word from the Lord because of the problems that arise in our lives, how much more do those who are hungry, homeless and hopeless, who are ill-clothed, with broken health, with no work and no money, who are angry or hurt or just feel downright no good, need to hear the news that Jesus saves from the guttermost to the uttermost.

This stigmatized woman with her bleeding condition, in the opinion of some persons, should not have even been out in public mixing with the crowd. How would people react to her if they noticed her emaciated body in their midst? However, for the opportunity of being blessed and healed by

Jesus, this woman was prepared to defy the crowd. Whether the crowd approved of her presence or not, she was not going to miss out on her blessing. Jesus is always deeply touched even by the simplest touch when faith is determined to defy the crowd and press its way to victory. It must not have been easy for this frail woman to press her way through the crowd to reach Jesus. Yet she was determined to make contact with the Savior. Jesus always pauses when his children don't allow obstacles and hindrances to stop them from reaching him. When, despite disappointments in the past and discouragement in the present, they press on anyhow.

All who have strayed need to find their way back to God. Somebody who has been discouraged, somebody who has stopped working in the church, or has started to hold back because she or he have been hurt, needs to make a new commitment. Jesus is passing by and we can't allow others to stop us from reaching out to touch him. He has healing for the heart, hurt, and body; he has the hope and the help; he has the forgiveness and cleansing that we need. We have to be prepared to say, "Whether I'm accepted by a certain crowd or not, I'm still coming to church; I'm still going to serve the Lord; I'm still going to work; I'm still going to sing; I'm still going to shout."

The woman of the story had a daring faith. To believe that only a touch can bring healing is a bold and daring proposition. Jesus always pauses in the presence of a daring faith. It takes a daring faith to tithe when bills are going up and real income is going down. It takes a daring faith to believe that no matter how long we've labored with our affliction or addiction or problem, we can still be delivered and healed. When the divorce rate is as high as it is, it takes a daring faith to believe that a relationship can work. And when things don't work out between people, it takes a daring faith to start over rather than to continue living a lie. When there are so many temptations and distractions, it takes a daring faith to say "I'm going to live single and holy."

What happens when a crowd-defying, determined, and daring faith meets a powerful and sensitive Savior? Healing happens and wholeness is given; salvation comes and Jesus pauses to ask "Who touched me?" The woman came forth and fell at Jesus' feet and told her story. Jesus looked at her and said, "Daughter, your faith has made you well; go in peace, and be healed of your disease."

It takes a daring faith to believe that no matter how long we've labored with our affliction or addiction or problem, we can still be delivered and healed.

He called her "daughter." She who had been cast out and shut off is called "daughter" by the Savior. I dare you to defy the crowd and reach out and touch the Lord because you are still his child. The world may write you off as a nobody and even the crowd around the church may shun you, but you are still a child of God.

"Who touched me?"

Jesus, one of your children has touched you. One of your lonely, needy, desperate, rejected, discouraged, weakened, broken children has touched you.

Chapter Six

Why Are You Doing This?

Mark 11:1-4

THIS CRUCIAL QUESTION, "WHY ARE you doing this?" was asked in a very specific context; however, its application to life and faith is much broader than the setting in which it was spoken. The context of this question was originally in the set of instructions that our Lord gave to two of the disciples regarding his entry into Jerusalem as a distinct prophetic act. We have all heard the saying, "I'd rather see a sermon than hear one any day." The prophets of old sometimes used various symbolic acts, or embodied in their own lives the message they were trying to convey. Thus, Isaiah walked stark naked through the streets of Jerusalem as a sign that the Assyrians would lead the Egyptians into captivity barefoot and naked, to their shame, and as a warning to the people of Israel not to entrust their deliverance to the Egyptians or any other nation, but to God.

The prophet Hosea married the prostitute Gomer who was unfaithful to him, and yet Hosea continued to be faithful to her. Hosea became a living parable of Israel's relationship with God. In spite of the many times and ways in which Israel had been unfaithful to the covenant relationship with God, God's love for Israel had been steadfast and enduring. The prophet Jeremiah remained celibate as a sign that the coming generation would be cut off from its heritage. He ruined a new linen waistcloth to demonstrate how Judah would be spoiled for not heeding God's word, and broke a vessel in the presence of the elders to show how Judah as a nation would be broken.

Thus, Jesus' entry into Jerusalem during the season of his last Passover on earth was a prophetic action that would show to those who had eyes to see more clearly than anything he could say to those who had ears to hear, that he was the Messiah. His entry into Jerusalem was a fulfillment of the messianic prophecy found in Zechariah 9:9, "Rejoice greatly, O daughter of Zion! Shout aloud, O daughter of Jerusalem! Lo, your king comes to you; triumphant and victorious is he, humble and riding on [a donkey], on a colt the foal of [a donkey]."

People had been discussing him among themselves and asking him who he was ever since he had first appeared on the Galilean frontier and in the Judaean wilderness. John the Baptist in a moment of doubt had sent him a message, "Are you he who is to come, or shall we look for another?" (Matt. 11:3). At that time Jesus demonstrated by his actions who he was. "Go and tell John what you hear and see: the blind receive their sight and the lame walk, lepers are cleansed and the deaf hear, and the dead are raised up, and the poor have good news preached to them. And blessed is he who takes no offense at me" (Matt. 11:4-6).

Some of the Jews had come to him at another time and said, "How long will you keep us in suspense? If you are the Christ, tell us plainly." Jesus answered, "I told you, and you do not believe. The works that I do in my Father's name, they bear witness to me; but you do not believe" (John 10:24-26*a*). Jesus answered their question by pointing to something that they could see.

Jesus' entry into Jerusalem was to be another living sermon of who he was, since the people had missed the others. Later that day when he dismounted from his donkey and went into the temple and chased out the extortionate money changers, that was another living sermon about who he was. In the Garden of Gethsemane when Peter severed the ear of the high priest's servant, Jesus restored the ear on the spot. That was another living sermon about who he was. That message of healing mercy and divine power did not turn the hearts of the angry mob. They proceeded with their purpose as if no miracle had happened in their midst.

When Jesus died on Calvary, God put on a cosmic demonstration; God initiated a heavenly action that told who Jesus was. At high noon the land became as dark as midnight. And as the preachers of my childhood used to say, "the earth began to reel and rock like a drunken man." Were the hearts of most of those present changed by what they saw? Except for one centurion on guard duty who declared, "Truly this man was the Son of God!" most went on their normal way as if nothing unusual had taken place before their very eyes. The soldiers at the foot of the cross continued to gamble for the clothes of Jesus and the crowd continued to mock, "If you are the Son of God, come down from the cross." When we look at the life and death of Jesus we see that it was essentially one continuous sermon that was not only preached, but lived. Everything that he said was backed up with deeds. People who lived during Jesus' time had the opportunity to see the best sermon that ever walked the face of the earth, and yet most people were not persuaded that Jesus was God's anointed. They continued to hold onto their personal, narrow, sincere but erroneous views of the Messiah.

People are no different now. Those who say that they would rather see a sermon than hear one any day must remember that unless their hearts and minds are open—as well as their eyes—then what they see won't make any difference anyway. God's word is being fulfilled in our midst every day. We see it and it still doesn't make us act any better or any differently. All around us we see evidence of sin and decadent lifestyles. We see lives that are wrecked by drugs, individuals destroyed by alcohol, people gasping with shortness of breath because of their failure to take care of the body as the temple of the Lord. Yet in spite of these living sermons of judgment we still persist in our damnable habits.

> *Those who say that they would rather see a sermon than hear one any day must remember that unless their hearts and minds are open—as well as their eyes—then what they see won't make any difference anyway.*

We see examples of Christ's transforming power. We see individuals who have been changed for the better by the power of their belief in Jesus Christ as Savior and Lord. We see people who are living examples of God's healing power. We see people who have bounced back from sorrow, setbacks, and tragedy with renewed strength because of their belief in a way-making God who does all things well, who sustains even as God perfects. We see how the church has made a difference in so many lives. Yet in spite of what we see, many of us are still not persuaded to try living fully for the Lord. We can have a minister living a sainted life in our midst. We can have a good companion far beyond our deserving. We can have persons of integrity, character, and good and correct faith in our lives, but if our minds are not in the right places, we will still be suspicious and distrusting, no matter what we see. A twisted mind will see life and people from a twisted perspective no matter how upright others try to be and indeed are. People who say that they'd rather see a sermon than hear one any day ought to also pray that the Lord will give them wisdom to understand and appreciate what they see, and then the courage to change in their lives whatever needs to be changed based upon what they see.

As Jesus prepared for another living prophetic sermon, he told two of the disciples to go to a nearby village. As they would enter it, they would find a colt tied, upon which no one had ever sat. They were to untie the colt and bring it to him. If anyone asked them what they were doing or questioned, "Why are you doing this?" they were to reply, "The Lord has need of it. . . . "

Why are you doing this? That's a very crucial question that every child of God must answer at one time or another. At some point all of us will be questioned about our actions as followers of Christ. Why are you doing this? Some companion or child will ask as we leave the house for church. They may not question why we go to work, or why we spend time with our friends. After all they like to spend time with theirs. But we will be questioned about our involvement in church. Why are you doing this? Curious neighbors, associates, or coworkers will ask when we invite them to attend church or to support various church functions, or when we turn down their invitations to socialize with them on Sundays.

Why are you doing this? Friends will ask when we don't go around the old hangouts, talk the same old trash anymore, and don't laugh at the same old jokes anymore. Sometimes they will feel as if we're breaking up the friendship. Why are you doing this? Some person will ask as we prepare to attend a church conference, retreat, or seek to deepen and develop ourselves spiritually. Why are you doing this? Some church members will ask when they see us tithing and making great financial pledges. Why are you doing this? Some church members who are not as diligent or faithful in their stewardship or discipleship will ask when they see us attending meetings and rehearsals, working hard and caring when nobody else, including the pastor, seems to care.

And sometimes we will ask ourselves the same question. Why are you doing this? Some usher will ask himself or herself while standing at the door trying to perform a service and someone who is rude and discourteous comes in with an attitude and takes the joy out of the usher's service. Why are you doing this? Someone in the kitchen will ask this as she or he is sweating over a hot stove while others are dressed up and sitting in church and enjoying worship. Why are you doing this? We'll ask ourselves when we volunteer our time and talents and are criticized and talked about; when we keep our word while others go back on theirs; when our efforts seem unappreciated, unrewarded, unrecognized, and under-valued. Why are we doing this? We'll ask ourselves when we are trying to live a good life and are still catching hell; when doing wrong seems to compensate with bigger and better dividends; and when God has either said no or seemed to have turned a deaf ear to our heartfelt prayers.

Why are you doing this? First Peter 3:15 tells us, "Always be prepared to make a defense to any one who calls you to account for the hope that is in you, yet do it with gentleness and reverence." How shall we answer the question, "Why are you doing this?"

"The Lord has need of it. . . . "

Why are we giving our dollar? Because the Lord has need of our little bit even as he needed the little boy's lunch of two fish and five barley loaves to feed the masses. Why are we giving our last two cents? Because the Lord needs our sacrifice to encourage and teach others even as he needed the examples of the widow who gave the two mites. Why are we giving whatever we have no matter how insignificant it may appear to be? Because the Lord has need of it, even as he needed a donkey for his triumphal entry into Jerusalem. Why are we singing in the choir? Because the Lord has need of our voice even as he needed the witness of the Samaritan woman that he met at Jacob's well so that she could spread the news about the living water she had found. Why are we faithful when others are not? Because in a time of betrayals, denials, and desertions, the Lord needs somebody to stand at the foot of the cross even as did John, the beloved disciple, and Mary, his mother. Why do we keep coming to church? Because the Lord needs somebody to carry on his work until he returns. But like Peter and the other disciples, we've failed the Lord, failed ourselves, and failed others. We need a word of forgiveness, restoration, comfort, and empowerment, so that the Lord can still get the glory out of our lives in spite of our past mistakes.

Occasionally we attend a theater and see a one-person play, but those are the exceptions rather than the rule. Most plays and movies have a number of persons in the cast. Some are lead actors, actresses, or stars with major roles. This person's performance is critical because a play or movie is made real by how well the star performs his or her role. No matter how good the script is, if the actors don't really star in their roles, the movie loses its punch. However, surrounding the stars are the supporting cast. They provide the setting and the background for the stars. They have to blend in with the action and perform their small parts in such a way that they take nothing away from the drama or the star's performance. Even though they don't get the glory, they still have a role to play and are part of the drama.

Redemption is not a one-person play, but an epic with a supporting cast of thousands and even millions of faithful believers and forerunners, some of whom died not having received the promise. He who is the Bright and Morning Star has the critical lead role because the whole play of redemp-

> *Redemption is not a one-person play, but an epic with a supporting cast of thousands and even millions of faithful believers and forerunners, some of whom died not having received the promise.*

tion depends upon his faithfulness, righteousness, and obedience to the well-written script and the way he consummates and perfects his part. On that first Palm Sunday, scene one of the final act of the drama of salvation was unfolding. Jesus had the leading role and all the eyes in Jerusalem were focused upon him as he acted out the fulfillment of messianic prophecy, as he gave them a living sermon that they could see. But surrounding him was the supporting cast. The disciples and others whose names we know were part of that cast. The unknown supporter who lent Jesus the donkey he rode upon was part of that cast. But surrounding them was a huge supporting cast of thousands who cried "Hosanna! Blessed is he who comes in the name of the Lord!" Palm Sunday would not have happened without the supporting cast because it was their shouts that shook the city.

Why are you doing this? Because the Lord needs a supporting cast and you are part of that supporting cast. Your role may not be major but you still have a part to play and you're still part of the redemption drama. That's why you're an officer: you're part of the supporting cast. That's why you're ushering: you're part of the supporting cast. That's why you're cooking in the kitchen: you're part of the supporting cast. That's why you're singing in the choir: you're part of the supporting cast. That's why you're teaching in Sunday school: you're part of the supporting cast. That's what it means to be a faithful church member: to be part of the supporting cast.

> *That's what it means to be a faithful church member: to be part of the supporting cast.*

Why are you doing this? There is yet another reason. In 1964 when the Civil Rights march from Selma to Montgomery, Alabama, was held, as a young college student I boarded a bus in St. Louis, Missouri, and rode all night long to be part of that great demonstration. I didn't have a major role to play. But I wanted to make my own personal witness and be one of the number that marched into Montgomery.

We do what we do in the service of the Lord first because we want to make our personal witness. The Lord has been good to us and brought us from a mighty long way, and the time has to come when we make our own witness. We have to tell our own story and praise and thank God for ourselves. But in addition, we know that there will be another triumphal entry into a new Jerusalem, and we just want to be in that number. When the four and twenty elders cast their crowns before him, we want to be in that number. When the cherabim, seraphim, and the four beasts cry out "Holy," we want to be in that number. When the angelic choirs begin to sing a new song, we want to be in that number. When those who have come out of the great tribulation, with robes washed in the blood of the lamb receive their "Well done!" we want to be in that number. When God wipes the tears away from the eyes of the faithful, we want to be in that number. When the hungry sit down at the welcome table, the thirsty drink from the river of life, and those who are sick find the tree whose leaves are good for the healing of the nations, we want to be in that number. But most of all when Jesus Christ, our Savior, is crowned Lord of all, we want to be in that number.

> When the saints go marching in,
> When the saints go marching in,
> Lord I want to be in that number,
> When the saints go marching in.

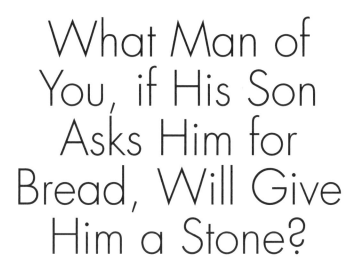

Chapter Seven

What Man of You, if His Son Asks Him for Bread, Will Give Him a Stone?

Matthew 7:9-11

THIS CRUCIAL QUESTION REMINDS US of a basic truth, which is this—God knows how to bless God's children. While we all affirm this truth, there are times when we may have to call it to remembrance. All of us have had the experience of earnestly asking God for something and having that request denied. Perhaps what we asked for was something that we felt we really desired, or even needed. Perhaps what we asked for, from our perspective, was a good thing and would harm neither ourselves nor anyone else. However, some of the things we perceive as being good for us are harmful for others, and God is not going to hurt someone else in order to give us the desires of our hearts. Certain requests, though, are good and are harmful to no one and are small things for a great God to do. Yet our request was denied and we were left mystified. We can't understand why an all-powerful, way-making God would not crack a small door to allow this good thing to happen to us.

In those moments of frustration, disappointment, and questioning, we would do well to listen to these crucial questions. "What man of you, if his son asks him for bread, will give him a stone? Or if he asks for a fish, will give him a serpent? If you then, who are evil, know how to give good gifts to your children, how much more will your Father who is in heaven give good things to those who ask him!"

Those who are parents know that, for the most part, we parent by trial and error. Those of us who come from good Christian homes and good Christian families try to rear our children in the manner in which we were reared. After all,

> ## Those who are parents know that, for the most part, we parent by trial and error.

the wisdom and guidance of our parents and our home training have served us well. However, parents often discover that even the most traditional and conservative among us cannot wholly transfer all of the rules by which we were raised to our children. For even though righteousness and eternal truth have not changed, although the Ten Commandments are still the Ten Commandments and not the ten suggestions, times have changed. Thus, our children will be tested in different ways as they try to apply the Commandments to their lives, than as we were tested when we were growing up.

When we were living in an age in which Sunday was respected as a special holy day and most retail stores were closed and much activity was curtailed, it was easier to teach children to respect Sundays as the Lord's Day than it is in an era in which everything is open on Sunday and young people can go just about every place, do almost anything, and buy just about everything that they can on any other day. Many of us stayed in church all day on Sunday because, first of all, our parents demanded it, and second, because that was the only place to go, and the only place to meet boys and girls. Not so today. It's easier to teach respect for Sunday as the Lord's holy day in an era when normal routines and work cease and when there are fewer distractions.

There was a time when pornography was a back-alley, backdoor, sleazy business that was not allowed to rear its obscene head in the light of day. Now it's a legitimate business operating on Main Street whose advertisements children can read on their way to school.

It's easier to keep track of our children when we're in a community where everyone basically knows everybody else, and everyone looks out for everyone else's children, than it is in a large metropolitan area where we may not know anything about the families of those that our children befriend. Our children learn more, are exposed to more, and mature faster than we did at their ages. People used to say that when a child was a fast learner that she or he was getting out of the way of a sibling that might be coming along. Now a child has to learn fast simply to keep up and survive, whether or not there is a sister or brother in the future.

Thus, parents these days must sometimes get their points across in ways that are different from the ways that our parents did. Often knowing when to yield and when not to yield is a judgment call we make by trial and error. Then parents often discover that what works with one child may not work with another. I'm always amazed by the fact that

Often knowing when to yield and when not to yield is a judgment call we make by trial and error.

two children can come from the same parents, live in the same household, be exposed to the same influences, and turn out totally different. Some children will cry when we raise our voices or our hands. Other children can be spanked, but these children will not drop a tear to save their lives. Sometimes we want to tell children with that kind of personality that if they would wise up and quit being stubborn and fake a tear they could save themselves and their parents a lot of aggravation. Of course, part of their personality makeup consists of their not giving other persons the satisfaction of seeing them cry. Parents learn through trial and error what works and what doesn't work with children.

As parents, or simply as adult role models, we recognize that we haven't been perfect. We haven't been bad, abusive, or irresponsible, but we've made some mistakes. Over the course of the years we've made some erroneous judgment calls. There were times when we were inconsistent in our rulings and prejudiced in our opinions. There were times when we yielded when we should have stood firm. There were other times when we stood firm when we could have yielded. We praise God that our children and young people who observed us when we were not aware turned out as well as they did.

Yet, as imperfect as we've been as parents or adult role models, as much as we've had to learn about guiding young people in an age different from the one of our youth, with all we've had to learn about the differing temperaments, moods, likes and dislikes of our respective children and what works or doesn't work for each of them, even we have sense enough not to give children stones when they ask for bread, and not give them serpents when they ask for fish. Even we know better than to do that. Let us receive courage from the words of Jesus. "If you then, who are evil, know how to give good gifts to your children, how much more will your Father who is in heaven give good things to those who ask him!"

If we, as imperfect, stumbling, and bumbling adults know how to bless children, how much more does our heavenly Father! God is too wise to make a mistake, and too just to do any wrong. How much more does God know how to bless us. If responsible and loving human parents would never disappoint children out of sheer meanness, how much more would our heavenly Father—who loved us so much that he allowed Jesus to die for our redemption—not withhold from us simply because he is able. If we, as parents, with our erroneous judgment and limited knowledge believe we know what is best for our children, how much more does our heavenly Father, whose judgment is perfect and whose wisdom and knowledge are beyond reproach, know what's best for us.

Human parents know their children. We know when they're ill. We know when they're hurting. We know when they're troubled. We know when they're hiding something. We know when they're afraid. We know when we've reached them and we know when we haven't. We know when their spirits are changing and are reflecting growth. We know when we must intercede because they have gotten in water too deep for them or when they have strayed from their course. How much more does our heavenly Father who made us in his own image and blew into us the breath of life, who put every blink in our eyelids, every beat in our hearts, the flow into our blood, who made every cell in our bodies, and colored every strand of hair upon our heads know all about us.

Our heavenly Father, our Divine Parent, knows when we're not well. He knows when we're hurting. He knows when we're lying and pretending to be something that we're not. He not only knows when we're hiding something, but he knows what we're hiding. He knows when we're afraid, and when our confidence is shaken. He knows when we're becoming stronger, and when we're getting weaker. He knows when he must intercede because we're in over our heads in sin, sorrow, sickness, or trouble. In other words, our heavenly Father knows just how much we can bear.

We know that he knows because somehow from somewhere we receive the strength to bear what we must. We may not know just how we're going to make it, but our heavenly Father does. He has power, from when he lit the sun and ten thousand other stars, to give us. He has love left over from Calvary to give us. He has anointing left over from the Day of Pentecost to bestow upon us.

Our heavenly Father knows how to bless us. He knew how to bless Moses at the Red Sea, the children of Israel during their wilderness wanderings, Daniel in the lions' den, and the three Hebrew boys in the fiery furnace. He knew how to keep Job when Satan tried to break him. He knew how to bless Paul and Silas at midnight in a prison cell and he knew how to renew John's faith on the lonely isle of Patmos. And when cruel men had crucified his Son, our heavenly Father knew how to bless him with such resurrection power that he would stoop no more and with such exaltation that at his name every knee must bow and every tongue confess him as Lord.

"What man of you, if his son asks him for bread, will give him a stone? Or if he asks for a fish, will give him a serpent? If you then, who are evil, know how to give good gifts to your children, how much more will your Father who is in heaven give good things to those who ask him!" God doesn't give stones for bread and serpents for fish. Sometimes in life we ask for what we think is a blessing, when it's actually a curse. There is an old legend in Greek mythology of Aurora who asked that Tithonus live forever. However, she forgot to ask that Tithonus stay forever young, so Tithonus grew older and older and older and older but could never die. His blessing became a curse.

We can accept without fear whatever we receive from the

hands of God. For whatever God gives nourishes and strengthens us. If he gives us a cross, then that cross lifts us. If he gives us a burden, then that burden blesses us. If he gives us tears, then those tears cleanse us. If he gives us enemies, then those enemies teach us. If he gives us discipline, then that discipline refines us. If he gives us trouble, then that trouble transforms us. If he gives us illness, then that illness illuminates us. We discover what we're really made of. If he gives us death, we're led to eternity.

> **We can accept without fear whatever we receive from the hands of God.**

Our heavenly Father knows how to take care of us. We don't know why God says "no" to some of our requests. But this we know: Our heavenly Father knows how to take care of us even when the doors of our desires don't open. We don't know why God allows the wicked to trouble us. But this we know: Our heavenly Father knows how to bless though hell's hounds rage. David testified, "Thou preparest a table before me in the presence of my enemies." We don't know why healing doesn't come for our sickness, but this we know: God will hold us with his very own hand, God's word will renew us, and God's spirit will commune with us even on a sickbed. We don't know why our loved ones had to die when they did, but this we know: Our heavenly Father will continue to make ways out of no ways for us. We don't know why we lost our jobs and when work will come, but this we know: Our heavenly Father who feeds the sparrows and clothes the lilies will take care of us. We don't know why our relationship or marriage had to end like it did, but this we know: Our heavenly Father will help us pick up the pieces of our broken hearts and start all over again. We don't know why this trouble has come into our lives, but this we know: Our heavenly Father is still in the blessing and prayer answering business, and he will see us through. Trouble doesn't last always. "Weeping may tarry for the night, but joy comes with the morning." He will see us through. Our heavenly Father knows how to bless us one and all.

How much greater is our heavenly Father's love than human love? If David could love his son after Absalom had rebelled against him and chased him from his throne, how much greater could the heavenly Father's love be than this? If the father of the prodigal son could celebrate when that son came back home even though his son had disgraced the family name and wasted his fortune in riotous living, how much greater could the heavenly Father's love be than this?

A father was baby-sitting his son in their tenth-story apartment one day. The mother had gone to work and the

> *If David could love his son after Absalom had rebelled against him and chased him from his throne, how much greater could the heavenly Father's love be than this?*

father was preparing breakfast. When he looked into the refrigerator he discovered that they were out of milk for cereal. He told his little boy, "Stay here and keep the door locked. Daddy's going to run to the store and I won't be gone long." The father was not gone any longer than fifteen minutes but when he tried to reenter his block, the street was filled with smoke and he saw people running and screaming. His heart almost stopped when he looked up the block and saw that his apartment building was engulfed in flames and smoke. While he was gone, the furnace had exploded and fire had quickly spread through the old tenement building. He could see his little boy standing on the ledge outside the window, not knowing what to do. The firemen had not yet been able to rescue his son and were worried about the building collapsing. The father broke through the barricade and ran up to the building and yelled to his son, "Jump! Daddy will catch you." The boy jumped and his father caught him. But the weight of the boy knocked the father down and he hit his head upon the curb of the sidewalk and broke his neck. With his dying breath he looked at his son and said, "When your mother comes home, tell her that I died in order that you might live."

How much greater is God's love than human love? On Calvary our heavenly Father gave Jesus the living bread come down from heaven, that we might live, that though our sins be as scarlet, they would be that way no more.

Chapter Eight

Are You the One?

Luke 7:18-19

THE SCRIPTURES TEACH AND ADMONISH us to be faithful, to endure, and to persevere; to hold out until we overcome and until our deliverance comes. There are times when we can bear our burdens without complaint or doubt, and when our faith strengthens as well as comforts. Then there are other times when we're not so sure. There are times when our faith gets a little shaky and we begin to wonder and doubt. Sometimes we are so buffeted by trials that we wonder if we're doing the right thing and if God is ever going to move. Sometimes Satan beats us so much that cracks and holes appear in what we thought was solid faith. Sometimes in an hour of weakness and trial, doubts can cause us to question some of the basic truths and beliefs that we had settled in our minds long ago. This, I believe, was the situation of John the Baptist in the text.

No one had been as bold or as zealous as John in proclaiming Jesus as the Messiah. It was John the Baptist who had stood on the banks of the Jordan River and proclaimed when he saw Jesus, "Behold, the Lamb of God, who takes away the sin of the world!" (John 1:29). This same John the Baptist who stooped to no human being; who spoke the truth no matter who it hit or how deeply it cut; who stood up to the king, the king's wife and family, the kings' court, and the religious establishment of his day; this same John who was so bold and brash with everyone else humbled himself at Jesus' request for baptism saying that "I should not be baptizing you, rather you should be baptizing me"; this same John the Baptist who had voluntarily taken a backseat to the ministry of Jesus saying, "he must increase, but I must decrease"; this same John who had been so sure of himself, who had been so supportive of Jesus, who had unreservedly heralded him as the Anointed of Israel, now began to have second thoughts.

Perhaps it was the peculiar circumstances in which John found himself that caused him to question something or someone whom he had been so sure of before. John was in prison awaiting the verdict of King Herod. He knew that the probability was great that he would either be locked up indefinitely or be killed. All of his life he had preached against sin, and had proclaimed that the judgment of God was upon Israel. He had preached that the Messiah would come. He had declared that Jesus was the promised one, the Anointed of God and the fulfillment of all prophecy. Now in the waning days of his life, now that he was imprisoned with no message or word of encouragement or comfort from Jesus, he began to question. It is difficult not to question when circumstances have our minds and spirits captive, and there is no word from Jesus.

This John who was accustomed to the desert with its wide-open spaces, clean air, and the sky for its roof, sat like a caged eagle, in an underground dungeon with the walls closing in upon him. In his loneliness and depression, doubt began to eat at his faith and he began to wonder if he had indeed been right. Was Jesus really who he thought he was? Had he been too hasty in proclaiming Jesus as the Messiah? He didn't have much time, consequently, before he went to his grave and he had to be assured that he hadn't made a mistake, that all would be well, and that his preaching and work had not been in vain. Thus he called two of his disciples and told them to find Jesus and tell him that "John the Baptist just wants to make sure, 'Are you the one? Are you he who is to come? Are you the Messiah? Are you the one who Isaiah referred to as Wonderful, Counselor, the Mighty God, the Everlasting Father, the Prince of Peace? Are you Daniel's Ancient of Days? Are you Ezekiel's wheel in the middle of a wheel? Are you Solomon's Rose of Sharon? Are you who we believe you are and hope you are, or shall we look for another?' "

Perhaps the reason John had second thoughts about Jesus was because of some of the reports that he had received about the Master. The Bible tells us that it was the disciples of John who brought him the report about all that Jesus was doing. We don't know if what they brought was fact or fiction. We don't know if what they told him was exactly what they saw and heard, or if they interpreted what they saw and heard and added to it what they wanted. We don't know if some of what John heard were rumors and stories floating around about Jesus. Rumors are dangerous things. A whispering campaign, though quiet, is a deadly campaign. I've seen how it can dampen enthusiasm and cause the weak to become discouraged and quit. I've seen how churches can be moving along in peace and unity, and then somebody starts circulating rumors about the preacher, or folks start

> *Rumors are dangerous things. A whispering campaign, though quiet, is a deadly campaign.*

whispering about one another's personal lives and business. If, like John, you're depressed already; if, like John, your faith is not as strong as it normally might be; if you're not careful, you will find yourself questioning and doubting people that you've known for years; people that you've worked with for years; people that you've trusted and felt secure about, and safe with, for years. Rumors can make you have second thoughts about things and people that you love, believe in, and have confidence in. Even though you have not seen that much firsthand (if anything at all), still you don't know who to believe or what to believe, and so like John you begin to question, "Are he and she all that we think they are? Are they really sincere? Can we put our trust and confidence in them? Are you the one, or shall we look for another?"

Perhaps one reason for John's second thoughts was that Jesus did not fit into John's preconceived notions of what the Messiah would be like, and what he would do. John preached a stern message of condemnation and judgment. He talked about the ax being laid to the root of the tree. He talked about a Messiah whose winnowing fork would be in his hand, who would clear the threshing floor, who would put the wheat into his granary, and burn the chaff in unquenchable fire. He called those who came to him a generation of vipers. John expected a Messiah who would condemn, who would mobilize the masses and free the land from Roman oppression. But Jesus came in an altogether different way. Instead of condemning sinners, he came saying that "the Son of Man is come to seek and to save that which is lost." He talked about the prodigal son coming

But Jesus came in an altogether different way. Instead of condemning sinners, he came saying that "the Son of Man is come to seek and to save that which is lost."

home to a gracious and all-forgiving father. He talked about
the good shepherd who searched for the lost sheep. Instead
of inciting the people to revolt, Jesus taught an entirely new
doctrine:

> "Blessed are the poor in spirit, for theirs is the kingdom of
> heaven.
> "Blessed are those who mourn, for they shall be comforted.
> "Blessed are the meek, for they shall inherit the earth.
> "Blessed are those who hunger and thirst for righteousness,
> for they shall be satisfied.
> "Blessed are the merciful, for they shall obtain mercy.
> "Blessed are the pure in heart, for they shall see God.
> "Blessed are the peacemakers, for they shall be called sons of
> God.
> "Blessed are those who are persecuted for righteousness'
> sake, for theirs is the kingdom of heaven.
> "Blessed are you when men revile you and persecute you
> and utter all kinds of evil against you falsely on my
> account. Rejoice and be glad, for your reward is great in
> heaven, for so men persecuted the prophets who were
> before you." (Matt. 5:3-12)

Instead of teaching vengeance and hate, Jesus taught,
"You have heard that it was said, 'You shall love your neigh-
bor and hate your enemy.' But I say to you, Love your enemies and pray for those who persecute you, so that you may
be children of your Father in heaven; for he makes his sun
rise on the evil and on the good, and sends rain on the
righteous and on the unrighteous" (Matt. 5:43-45 NRSV).

Thus, as John sat imprisoned, with Jesus acting so totally
different from John's expectations, with teachings that were so
radically different from what John expected to hear, and doing
none of the things he expected a Messiah to do, John grew a
little impatient and doubtful: "When is Jesus going to start
moving? When is he going to blast our enemies? When is he

going to slay the wicked? When is the day of God's holy destruction going to begin? Maybe he's not going to do any of it. Maybe I've been wrong about him. Jesus, before I die, I've got to know, are you the one, or shall we look for another?"

John may have had his doubts and hang-ups, but instead of brooding over his concerns and letting them fester in his soul, as some of us do, he sought to do something about them. He placed his concerns before Jesus. When Jesus heard John's questions, he didn't get offended; he didn't argue or try to prove his messiahship. He simply continued to do the work of the Lord. And in that same hour he cured many diseases and plagues and evil spirits. Then he turned to John's disciples and said, "Go and tell John what you have seen and heard."

You don't have to try to prove to people that you are what you claim to be—that you are sincere, that you've been born again, that you're a child of God. Just do the work of the Lord, and the work you do will speak for you. Just live the life, and the life you live will tell whether or not you have anything to say. Just go serve God, serve humanity, and

> You don't have to try to prove to people that you are what you claim to be—that you are sincere, that you've been born again, that you're a child of God.

the service you give will tell its own story about who you are and what you are all about. "A sound tree cannot bear evil fruit, nor can a bad tree bear good fruit. . . . Thus you will know them by their fruits" (Matt. 7:18-20).

"Tell John what you have seen and heard. Tell him that the blind see clearly; the lame walk without a limp; lepers are cleansed and purified; the deaf hear again; the dead come back to life. And the poor, the bruised, those without hope, have good news preached to them. Tell John that grace, mercy, love, forgiveness, deliverance, and salvation have come. Tell John the kingdom has begun to dawn. It might not be according to his expectations, but God is still at work. Whenever eyes are opened to the goodness of God, the kingdom has come. Whenever ears are unstopped to the hearing of God's word, the kingdom has come. Whenever filthy lives are cleansed by the precious blood of the Lamb, the kingdom has come. Whenever feet are made to walk the straight path, the kingdom has come. Whenever dead hopes are resuscitated, whenever dead spirits are revived, whenever dead faith is reawakened, whenever dead courage finds strength again, the kingdom has come. Whenever those who feel like they have no reason to live, whenever the discouraged and those without hope hear good news, the kingdom of God has come. Tell John blessed is he who doesn't lose faith in me—who holds on through hardship and trial, sorrow and pains. Whether it's in a prison or sickbed, blessed is he who doesn't lose faith, who does not faint, but waits to see the goodness of the Lord in the land of living."

Yes, sometimes like John, we too become impatient. Sometimes, we wonder Where is God? Sometimes we want God to move, and we want God to move "right now." A woman whose only son was killed in an automobile accident was told by her pastor to have faith and trust God. "Trust God?" she replied. "Where was God when my son was killed?" The preacher told her, "The same place he was on that afternoon when his only begotten son was crucified on Calvary. His love was constant and was at work in the midst of a seemingly cruel, unjust, tragic world in order to bring forth from the ashes of a darkened Good Friday, the glorious victory and stunning resurrection of an Easter Sunday morning." Sometimes when trials come to our lives we want God to remove the thorns and take away the pain and suffering "right now." When our Savior doesn't come when we think he should, and in the way we think he should, we're tempted to ask, "Are you the one, or shall we look to alcohol, sin, cynicism, vengeance, or bitterness. Shall we look for another?" All around us we hear conflicting voices and we don't know who and what to believe.

Many times out of our frustrations, our doubts, our trials, and our impatience we cry out, "Are you the one or shall we look for another?" But the Master speaks and says, "Before you doubt me, look at what I've already done for you. When you were in sin, I redeemed you. When you had done wrong, I forgave you. When you were unworthy, I loved you. When you were a captive to sin, I set you free. When you were sick, I healed you. When you were out-of-doors, I took you in. When you didn't know where to go or what to do, I showed you. When your way was blocked, I

> *All around us we hear conflicting voices and we don't know who and what to believe.*

made a way out of no way. When your heart was heavy, I gave you comfort. When you didn't have a job, I opened up one for you. When your mind was disturbed, I gave you peace. I helped you raise those children. And when they strayed it was I who kept your hopes alive. Do you think your marriage could have lasted without me? I'm the one who gave you strength to forgive and not give up. When you wanted to get an education, I made it possible. When you needed a mother and a father, I was there. When you needed a friend, I gave you one; when you needed help I sent you some. And as I told John, I tell you, blessed is the one who does not take offense to me. Blessed are those who do not lose their faith. Blessed are those who endure to the end; who wait for their change to come; who fight the good fight of faith; who having done all, stand anyhow."

I don't know about you but I know that he's the one. "For God has done great things for me, He opened doors I could not see; I'll trust His word, for His word is true; God has already done what He said He would do."

I know he's the one, "I can tell the world about this; I can tell the nation about this; tell them that Jesus has come; tell them that the Comforter has come; and He's brought joy, joy, joy to my soul."

I know he's the one, for he's real in my soul. "So many people doubt Him, I can't live without Him/That is why I love Him so, He's so real to me."

"Are you the one or shall we look for another?" "Yes he is the one . . ."

> There's not a friend like the lowly Jesus,
> No, not one! no, not one!
> None else could heal all our soul's diseases,
> No, not one! no, not one!
>
> Jesus knows all about our struggles,
> He will guide till the day is done;
> There's not a friend like the lowly Jesus,
> No, not one! no, not one!

Chapter Nine

Do You Want to Be Healed?

| John 5:6 |

TODAY'S CRUCIAL QUESTION SEEMS A bit strange at first. Why would Jesus ask a man who had been lame for thirty-eight years if he wanted to be healed? Why would the Lord ask someone if he or she wanted to be healed when the person was already at the pool believing it would heal the affliction? Why would the Master ask someone if he or she wanted to be healed when the person had been faithfully coming to the place of healing, day after day, week after week, and year after year?

Perhaps Jesus knew that sometimes, in spite of our actions and our words, we have secretly given up on ourselves or our situation, and really don't believe we can be, or are going to be, healed, helped, heard, saved, or made whole. Sometimes we can habitually go through certain actions, routinely participate in certain rituals or procedures, and customarily say certain things without really believing in what we're doing or saying.

> *Perhaps Jesus knew that sometimes, in spite of our actions and our words, we have secretly given up on ourselves or our situation, and really don't believe we can be, or are going to be, healed, helped, heard, saved, or made whole.*

Sometimes, like Samson rising from Delilah's lap after she had cut his hair while he slept, we may have lost our faith or our strength without knowing it. Thus the question "Do you want to be healed?" helps us to confront ourselves and ask ourselves, truthfully and honestly, do we still have the desire, first, for healing; and second, do we still have the faith that makes that desire a possibility? Have we built a tent around our problem that is an impermanent structure and implies that one day we're going to pack up and move on? Or have we built a house around our affliction that is a permanent structure and says that this spot is the place of our habitation? Someone has said that we could endure the terrors of hell if we believed that we would one day get out, and that the suffering would only last for a season. Some of us feel that we're in living hells because we've been like we are and where we are for so long that, short of death, we've given up hope of ever getting out.

There are various reasons for the inherent contradiction between going to the pool, on the one hand, and having secretly given up hope for healing, on the other. Sometimes our faith is worn down by the sheer length of time we've had the problem. Thirty-eight years is a long time to put up with anything. Some of us have lived with our affliction for so long that we don't know how to be any other way but miserable. We've complained about our problems, our ailments, our families, our jobs, and our churches for so long that all we know how to do is complain. We've begged for so long that begging is all we know. We've been crying poor for so long that even when we've been abundantly blessed, we're still crying poor, acting poor, and living poor.

We're more inclined to frown than to smile, find it easier to criticize than to congratulate, and tend to look for what's wrong rather than for what's right. Even when some of us make an effort at being positive we still end up sounding negative. A person once looked into the mirror and said, "I'm tired of all of these negative feelings that I've been having about myself, about others, and about life. I'm going to think some positive thoughts. I'm going to start believing in myself. I'm going to think all of these positive things even though they probably won't help me much or do me much good."

Sometimes our faith is worn down because of the number of times that our hopes have been raised and then frustrated. Who knows how many times the man had been brought to the pool with raised hope that he would be healed that day? Who knows how many times he had been close but not close enough to be the first to step into the water when it was troubled? It's hard to keep one's faith up when we've been disappointed and frustrated time after time.

> *Sometimes our faith is worn down because of the number of times that our hopes have been raised and then frustrated.*

Thus, to keep our faith from being shattered altogether we start lowering our expectations. Hear us as we say, "I'll give this preacher or this church a chance, but I won't be surprised if this experience turns out negatively just like the others. "I'll give this person a chance, but I just know that sooner or later she's going to mess up." Some of us have been knowing people, watching people, and living with people for years, and still are afraid to trust them. "I'll try this new doctor or hire a new lawyer, but this person probably won't be able to do any more than the others." "My companion and I had a good talk and reached an understanding, but we've done that before so I really don't expect things to change much." Well, when we expect little from other people and from ourselves, that's usually what we get, and that's all we're going to see even when much is happening. "I'm going to try sending her to a new school or they're going to put him into another class or she's going to move to another department, but I'll be surprised if the results are any better." "I'm going to continue praying, even though nothing is happening."

First of all we don't know all that may be happening. We don't know what things God is setting in place. We don't know whose heart God is touching. We don't know how, when, or where God is working, but know this: God is working all the time. God never sleeps, God's watchful eye never shuts, and God's grace, power, and love never go on vacation. Second, let us remember that we are not simply instructed to "pray without ceasing" but to pray believing.

I know it's hard to be positive in the face of repeated failures and disappointments, but hold on to your hope and don't give up. If we're children of God we should never lower our expectations, because with God all things are possible. We must continue expecting God to do great things and to produce mighty works in our lives. What we desire may or may not happen, but the possibility is there if we don't give up. However, when we lose hope we shut the door in possibility's face.

"Do you want to be healed?" There are some things in life we have to want for ourselves. Teachers may want their students to learn ever so much, but those students must want to learn for themselves. How have so many Blacks come from the South and other places, from schools that were separate, unequal, and underfunded, and become honor students and National Merit scholars, and then competed with Whites in major colleges and universities and later in the marketplace? They wanted to learn. Before we criticize the schools too severely for all they're not doing with our children, we must realize that our children need to make up their minds that they want to learn.

We must decide we're going to be something or somebody ourselves. Mother or father, sister or brother, friend or companion, the preacher or the teacher, can't make that decision for us. If we don't want to be anything, then no

> There are some things in life we have to want for
> ourselves.

matter what opportunities present themselves to us, they will
be like pearls before swine; they will be wasted on us and
we'll become nothing. And if we want to be something and
do something worthwhile, then no matter what obstacles are
set before us, we'll find a way to deal with them or God will
help us or the Holy Spirit will direct us in how to handle
them, and we'll become something and accomplish something anyhow. I once heard a preacher of my childhood say
"Aim for the moon, and if you fall among the stars, don't
worry about it, because you will still be on high ground."

We run from doctor to doctor, hospital to hospital, use
prescription after prescription, and pray for miracles in vain
if we haven't really decided that we want to be healed. It's
good to have other folks pray for us, but we have to decide
ourselves that we want to live holy. Before we can turn our
backs upon temptation and change our lifestyles, we must
decide that we are serious about holiness. We should pray
for unsaved or unchurched loved ones, but at some point
they must decide for themselves that they want to be saved.
Before we can live clean and sober, free from drugs and
alcohol, we have to decide that is what we want to do.

"Do you want to be healed?" our crucial question challenges us to decide what kind of life we want to have. The
lame man answered Jesus' questions by saying, "Sir, I have no
man to put me into the pool when the water is troubled, and
while I am going another steps down before me." That was a
very touching story and an interesting explanation as to why
the man hadn't been healed. The only problem with his statement was that it didn't answer Jesus' question. The Master
didn't ask the lame man about who did what to him or who

stepped into the water before him. He didn't ask the lame man about his background, or his past disappointments, frustrations, and failed attempts. As nosy as some of us are, we might take the time to ask all those questions, but not Jesus. He asked a simple question that required a simple yes or no answer, and that question was "Do you want to be healed?"

This day, right now, Jesus is knocking on the door of somebody's heart and he is asking one simple question. We don't need to give the Lord a lot of answers to unasked questions. He's not asking us to give him some long, drawn out, hearts and flowers story about who did what to us, who talked about us, who doesn't like us, or who won't work with us. He is not asking us about how we got into our condition, or how we allowed ourselves to get into such a position. He isn't asking us how long we've been like we are and how many times in the past we've tried to get right, and failed. He's not even asking us about how many opportunities for healing and salvation we've let go by, and why. And he's certainly not asking us about anyone else's business, faults, and failures. Jesus sees our condition, knows what we need, and has what we need. He's just asking us to give a simple "yes or no" answer to the question he is asking, "Do you want to be healed?"

Jesus told the man to, "Rise, take up your pallet, and walk." If we want to be healed, we're going to have to do something ourselves. The Lord didn't pull the man up or prop the man up or pick the man up. He only told him to "rise." He didn't slap the man. He didn't even touch the man. He just spoke a word of healing to him. The man had to have enough faith and submissiveness to obey Jesus' word. He had to want healing badly enough, he had to be desperate enough to obey Jesus' word even when he was commanded to do what had seemed impossible for him. Do we want healing badly enough? Are we desperate enough for salvation to obey Jesus' word even when he commands us to do difficult things, some of which seem to be impossibilities for us?

Jesus told the man to take up the pallet that he had been lying upon. Those who have been healed ought not be empty-handed. What are we carrying? Some people carry bitterness from the past. Some people carry excuses for not doing more than they're doing. Some people carry stones for throwing at their neighbors. Jesus told us what to carry. He told us, "If any man would come after me, let him deny himself and take up his cross and follow me" (Matt. 16:24).

Take the pallets that once held us, from which we could not rise, and carry them in our hearts as our testimony to what the Lord has done for us. The sickness, the drugs and drinks, the failures, weaknesses, and mistakes of the past, from which we could not rise become the testimonies that we

Are we desperate enough for salvation to obey Jesus' word even when he commands us to do difficult things, some of which seem to be impossibilities for us?

carry in our hearts about how the Lord can raise us. We can tell others, "If you don't believe that God's power is real, let me show you my pallet. Let me sing my song of praise. Let me tell my story of victory. Let me give my witness about how Jesus saves from the guttermost to the uttermost."

Jesus told the man to "Walk!" Walk by faith. Walk with your head up, praising and glorifying God. Some people may not understand why you walk like you do, but you know what the Lord has done for you. Some people may not believe your witness, but keep on walking, because you know that you've been raised. Walk by the grace of God. Walk in Jesus' name. Walk by the power of the Holy Spirit. Walk and know that you'll never walk alone.

Do You Also Wish to Go Away? . . . To Whom Shall We Go?

John 6:66-69

THINGS HAD BEEN GOING VERY WELL for Jesus. Everywhere he went, he drew large crowds. People were eager to see him, hear him, and observe his mighty works. They wanted to touch and be touched by him. People seemed to hang on his every word and take notice of his smallest action. According to John's account of his ministry, when Jesus had gone to Jerusalem to observe the Passover, many saw his mighty works and believed in his name. So many had come to be baptized by his disciples that the numbers exceeded those who had come to John the Baptist. Not only in bustling Jerusalem, but in rural Galilee, crowds had flocked to him. Even in reprobate Samaria, people heard him gladly and believed.

Through all of this excitement Jesus had remained relatively calm and unmoved by his popularity. Jesus knew that people were attracted to him for various reasons. There were those who wanted something from him. There were those who were curious about him. There were those who followed any new fad for a while. There were those who were trying to trip him in his words and find fault with his actions. There were those who believed that Jesus had more potential than anyone who had come along in years for freeing his people from Roman rule. Jesus was wise enough to know what to do and say to keep a crowd. He knew how to give people what they wanted. He knew how to exploit the emotions of those who were vulnerable as well as take advantage of the sincerity and commitment of the faithful. He knew how to satisfy the wondering of the curious. He even knew how to be so vague and noncommittal that he could forever elude and frustrate his enemies. What was important to Jesus, however, was not that people simply followed him, but that they followed him for the right reasons. We can follow Jesus, we can come to church and serve and work in the church for the wrong reasons, as well as the right ones. What was important to him was not that people heard his words and quoted them, but

> *What was important to Jesus, however, was not that people simply followed him, but that they followed him for the right reasons.*

that they understood them. For it is possible to hear and quote without understanding. What was important to Jesus was not that people simply observed his works, but that they understood the salvation that they represent and to which they pointed. It is possible to be present, to observe, to be a part of, and still not know what's going on.

Therefore, Jesus was not hesitant about answering the questions that were put to him and was completely honest about himself and the nature of the way in which he invited people to walk. Jesus knew that his teaching would be difficult for some to understand and impossible for others to accept and believe. However, he didn't try to hide anything about either the difficulties, or the rewards of the life and discipleship that he offered. Even if it meant losing a potentially valuable disciple like a rich young ruler, along with his resources, Jesus was always completely up front and out front about the requirements of the kingdom. There were no hidden clauses in his call and no fine print in his gospel; whether or not people understood him, Jesus repeatedly stated in clear language what he was about and where he was going.

One day, during the height of his popularity when talk and expectations were at their greatest about making him an earthly king of time and place, Jesus delivered one of his most difficult and unpopular messages—one that confounded a number of those who had been excited about him and had been following him. It was after the mighty miracle of the feeding of the five thousand with two fish and five barley loaves when Jesus' popularity seemed to be never ending that our Lord presented himself not as a victorious conqueror, but as an obedient suffering servant who would give his life as a ransom for many. Jesus talked about those who would follow him, eating his flesh and drinking his blood. For those who had seen our Lord as some rising star to whom they could attach themselves and profit thereby, for those who lacked spiritual insight, who dealt only with that which was on the surface, Jesus' teaching about giving his life, with others eating his flesh and drinking his blood, was a hard and difficult message to receive.

Let us never forget that although Jesus' message was good news, and although we are called to live a life of grace under God, Jesus still had some hard and difficult admonitions. Jesus said: "Love your enemies and pray for those who persecute you." That's a hard saying. If we don't believe that it's hard, just try living it. "Blessed are you when men revile you and persecute you and utter all kinds of evil against you falsely on my account. Rejoice and be glad, for your reward is great in heaven, for so men persecuted the prophets who were before you." That's a hard saying. If we don't believe it's difficult, wait until people begin to beat on us for standing for right and see if we feel either blessed or much like rejoicing. "Judge not, that you be not judged. For with the judgment you pronounce

> Let us never forget that although Jesus' message was good news, and although we are called to live a life of grace under God, Jesus still had some hard and difficult admonitions.

you will be judged, and the measure you give will be the measure you get." That's a hard saying. If we don't believe it's difficult, let us try knowing people's weaknesses without being judgmental and overly critical of them. Where would any of us be if God judged as harshly as we judge one another? If the measure we gave was the measure we received? Thank God for grace and mercy that is everlasting to everlasting. Many of Jesus' followers found certain of his admonitions and teachings too hard and difficult, and walked with him no more.

There were those who didn't understand what Jesus was saying and didn't stay around long enough to find out. With the first disappointment they walked away. How many of us are faithful when things suit us, but when the first difficulty arises or the first disappointment comes are ready to throw our hands up and give up? The first time the preacher disappoints or does or says something we don't understand, we are quick to say, "I told you that he or she could not be trusted and that he or she was just like all the rest." The first time our prayers don't get answered the way we want we are quick to say, "My God, my God, why have you forsaken me?" Some of us become discouraged so easily and so quickly. It's almost as if we are just looking for a reason to quit or resign, to leave the church, to stop giving, to stop working or servicing, or to break the promises and vows we made to the Lord. We hear and don't understand, our feelings get hurt, we become confused and we don't stay around long enough to get an understanding. Rather, we take our marbles and run home the first time we don't get our way, the first time our names are not called or our contributions overlooked, the first time somebody makes us mad, the first time we are falsely accused and criticized, the first time the preacher does something we don't like, the first time we hear something we don't agree with, the first time God does something or allows something to happen that we don't understand. We walk away in disgust with broken hearts, broken spirits, and broken faith.

There were those who walked away not because they didn't understand what Jesus was saying, but because they understood all too well what Jesus was saying. They understood all too well the implications and ramifications of Jesus' message both for him and for them if they continued to follow him. They

> *There were those who walked away not because they didn't understand what Jesus was saying, but because they understood all too well what Jesus was saying.*

understood that they would have to change their attitudes and adopt new values. They understood that they would have to make some sacrifices and take some risks for what they believed. They understood that if they followed Jesus too closely that the same thing that happened to him could happen to them. For, after all, no servant is greater than his master nor is the one who is sent greater than the one who sends. If they saw Jesus rejected and mistreated for righteousness' sake, could they or his followers expect any better treatment? They were not ready to deny themselves or take up any crosses and follow in the way of holiness, the way of sacrifice, the footsteps of Jesus. Consequently, they walked with him no more.

As many of those who had walked with him turned their backs to walk away from him, Jesus turned to the twelve, those whom he had called to be his special companions and asked, "Do you also wish to go away?" That's the searching question that Jesus still asks each of us and each of us must answer this question for ourselves. When others, for whatever reason—your friends, family, coworkers, and those whom you respect and look up to—drop by the wayside, quit, resign, or leave, "do you also wish to go away?" There will be times when following Jesus will not be easy. We want to understand the mysterious working of the hand of God on our lives and the sometimes seemingly callous and cruel dealings of God with us. In those times Jesus has a searching question for us, "Will you stay with me or do you also wish to go away?"

There will be times when we won't get the cooperation that we should. Our programs might fall short of our expectations and our best won't be good enough. In those moments of discouragement Jesus has a searching question for us, "Will you stay with me, or do you also wish to go away?" Sometimes vicious people who have nothing better to do but be envious and who don't know how to do anything better, will attempt to undermine our character and spread rumors about us. However, in those times of hurt and pain Jesus has a searching question for us, "Will you stay with me or now that the going has gotten a little rough and tough, do you also wish to go away?" When we're not reelected or reappointed to office and we're feeling angry and vindictive, Jesus has a searching question for us: "Will you stay with me or now that you don't have your office or your power base, do you also wish to go away?" When misunderstandings arise and tempers flare, and our patience runs out and we are pushed to our breaking point, before we break up or break out or break down, Jesus has a searching question for us, "Will you stay with me through misunderstandings, or do you also wish to go away?" Sometimes we will be criticized when we're doing the best we can by those who are doing nothing but talking. However, in those moments when we are closest to walking out and letting the faultfinders, busybodies, know-it-alls, and scoffers take control and make a bigger mess, Jesus has a searching question for us, "Will you stay with me, or do you also wish to go away?" When Satan has taken the joy out of our service and our worship, Jesus has a searching question for us, "Will you stay with me, or do you also wish to go away?"

When Jesus asked this question of the disciples, Peter spoke up. There were times when Peter spoke out of turn, when he was loud and wrong. But this time Peter's answer was sufficient because it came from his heart. Jesus' question came from the loneliness of his heart as he saw a number of his followers walk away. Peter's answer came from the fullness of his heart as he thought about what Jesus had meant to him and the other disciples. Questions of faith, commitment, and discipleship must ultimately be answered with the heart. Our minds can only take us so far; rationality and logic can only take us so far. At some point only the heart can speak, only

> *Questions of faith, commitment, and discipleship must ultimately be answered with the heart.*

the heart can respond to the word and the Spirit of God. Peter answered from his heart, "Lord, to whom shall we go? You have the words of eternal life; and we have believed, and have come to know, that you are the Holy One of God."

The first part of Peter's answer is a question that each of

us ought to ask ourselves when we think about going away. To whom shall we go? God may do some things or allow some things to happen that we don't understand, but to whom shall we go? The historic church, preachers, or church members may be imperfect, but to whom shall we go? What other groups of imperfect human beings have been blessed with the presence, the anointing, and the power of God's spirit, as we have? To whom shall we go?

Is there anyone who can help us, one who understands our hearts when the thorns of life have pierced us till we bleed? One who sympathizes with us, who in wondrous love imparts just the very, very blessing that we need?

> Yes, there's One! only One!
> The blessed, blessed Jesus, He's the One!
> When afflictions press the soul,
> When waves of trouble roll,
> And you need a Friend to help you, He's the One.

Shall we turn to insensitive and unfeeling human governments who are ruled by politics rather than by justice and morality? Shall we turn to companies who are ruled by profits to safeguard our best interests? Shall we turn to other faiths and sects who have the same imperfections and faults, if not more so, than we have? To whom shall we go when problems arise in our families, when tensions develop between husband and wife and misunderstandings arise between parent and child? To whom shall we go as single persons trying to make it by ourselves? To whom shall we go when ways need to be made out of no ways?

To *whom* shall we go. Not to *what*. Not to various "isms" such as materialism, not to false highs from drinks and drugs or power, but to whom? Only a sufficient relationship with one person has the answer we need and we know who that person is. Peter told Jesus, "You have the words of eternal life." You have the word of salvation for all of life's Samaritan women at Jacob's well and for all of life's tax collection from the Zacchaeuses. You have word of deliverance for those possessed by legions of demons. You have word of forgiveness for condemned thieves and those caught in sin. You have word of cleansing for the lepers. You have word of healing for the sick, and word of resurrection for the dead. You not only have word of life for this age, you have word of eternal life.

"And we have believed, and have come to know, that you are the Holy One of God." When we first started following you we believed, now we know. When you first called us we believed that you could make us fishers of persons, now we know you can, based on our own experience with you. I may not be able to answer all the questions about my faith, but based on my own experience I can give a sufficient answer. I know what God can do. I not only know that the Lord laid his hand upon me, I know that Lord keeps his hand upon me. He woke me up this morning, he brought me here this day, he will guide me when I leave this place. I know he loves me. I don't know why he does, but I know he cares. I know his grace is sufficient. I know that if you stay with him, then he'll stay with you when the world walks away from you. I know he heals, restores, makes ways, forgives, saves, sanctifies, and satisfies to the uttermost. I know he's the Holy One of God.

"Will you also go away?" That's a searching question. I don't have a perfect answer, but I have a sufficient answer, "To whom shall we go?"

Chapter Eleven

Wretched Man That I Am! Who Will Deliver Me?

Romans 7:24-25a

THIS WEEK AS I AGONIZED OVER this message my mind focused in on two very special men in my life. One is an individual whom I know intimately on the one hand, yet he is a mystery and an enigma to me on the other. Sometimes I think I know him like the palm of my hand, and at other times I think I don't know him at all, even though I have known and been close to him all of my life. I've watched him grow physically, spiritually, and emotionally as he has journeyed from infancy to manhood. I've seen him in his successes and failures, and have shared with him the thrill of his triumphs and the agony of his defeats. I've been with him through all of his struggles; I know his fears and his faith, his vices and his virtues, his weaknesses and his strengths. This person is one who at once makes me proud and ashamed. This person is one that I sometimes love and sometimes loathe. One of the individuals that I was led to focus upon this week is the man I see when I look into the mirror.

Socrates said, "The unexamined life is not worth living." God's word is worth reading because it consistently forces us to examine ourselves. God's glory is worth beholding because when we would become self-righteous, it makes us realize how far short of perfection we fall. God's greatness is worth remembering because it serves as a reminder of our own potential as a creation of God. Others are worth keeping in our perspective because they help us to come to grips with our selfishness. The needs of others are worth our attention because they safeguard our inclination to take our blessings for granted.

This crucial question is important because it raises for us the issue of self-examination. This important question today comes out of the throes of Paul's own self-examination. One of the reasons that Paul constantly grew in grace, one of the reasons that his witness was so effective was found in his willingness to look honestly at himself. A number of us pretend to be more—more righteous, more sincere, more intelligent, more affluent, more generous, more committed, or more honest—than we actually are. However, when I read the writings of Paul, I am amazed at his openness in confronting his own struggles and weaknesses.

A number of us pretend to be more—more righteous, more sincere, more intelligent, more affluent, more generous, more committed, or more honest—than we actually are.

The passage from which this crucial question comes is a case in point. Listen to Paul as he talks about his difficulties with the man in the mirror. He writes: "I do not understand my own actions. . . . I can will what is right, but I cannot do it. For I do not do the good I want, but the evil I do not want is what I do. . . . So I find it to be a law that when I want to do right, evil lies close at hand. For I delight in the law of God, in my inmost self, but I see in my members another law at war with the law of my mind and making me captive to the law of sin which dwells in my members. Wretched man that I am! Who will deliver me from this body of death?"

Like Paul, many of us find that the man or woman, boy or girl, we see in the mirror is one of our greatest resources, as well as our greatest challenge. All of us have persons in our lives who don't like us, and we, as well, have those who frankly we could do without—persons who intimidate or make us feel insecure, those who get on our nerves, or who cloud up a bright sunshiny day. However, I've discovered that if I can keep the man in the mirror correct, I can handle anyone. Often, our judgment of others, our perception and evaluation of others, is based upon what we see when we look into the mirror. If we feel good about what we see in the mirror then we will not be intimidated by, or fearful or jealous of others. However, if we do not feel good about what we see in the mirror, anyone can manipulate us.

People who are always picking others apart do not like what they see when they look in the mirror. If they liked what they saw in the mirror, it would not be necessary to pick everybody and everything apart to feel better about themselves. I once had a church member who found fault with just about everything I did. I could never do anything to please him and if I ever did, he was suspicious of my motive. He was negative and mean-spirited and would talk about me everywhere he went and to anyone who would listen. Of course, in all fairness to the brother, he not only talked about me, he talked about a number of people, as most gossipers do. Gossipers very seldom talk about one person only. Someone came to me and said, "What did you do to that brother? He sure dislikes you." I told him, "First, I don't know what, if anything, I've done to him. Second, his problem is not that he doesn't like me, but that he doesn't like himself." Because he doesn't like what he sees when he looks into the mirror, he resents anyone who embodies what he isn't or anyone who represents what he would like to see when he looks into the mirror.

All of us have problems. However, I have discovered that our ability to handle our problems is directly related to how we feel about what we see in the mirror. If what we see in the mirror is weakness and is out of focus, then we will struggle with every molehill, and our next step is our limit. However, if what we see in the mirror is positive and in focus, not even the sky is the limit. Yes, the person in the mirror is also our greatest challenge—not that person or the several individuals who cause us so much grief, not those we consider obstacles to our happiness; not that problem that we just can't seem to solve—but the man or woman in the mirror is our greatest challenge.

What do you see when you look in the mirror? Are you pleased or saddened? Do you see strength or weakness? If we are not pleased with what we see in the mirror, then no matter what we do, where we go, who we meet, or the company we keep, we will never be happy. When Socrates was

> *What do you see when you look in the mirror? Are you pleased or saddened? Do you see strength or weakness?*

asked why a certain man was the way he was, the philosopher replied that his problem was that "wherever he goes [he] takes himself with him."

Most of us are familiar with the television commercial that advertises a certain vegetable juice. In this commercial people are looking at a world that looks slanted. The world, however, is not slanted, the people are out of focus because they are supposedly deficient in the vitamins that the juice being advertised provides. The message of the commercial is simple: The world isn't altogether out of focus; we are. If we want the world to look straight, we must begin by straightening ourselves up.

Michael Jackson made this point in one of his songs titled "The Man in the Mirror." The lyrics describe one who looked upon a world of hungry children on the streets without enough to eat, and homeless persons with no place to lay their heads, who reaches the conclusion that the place to begin setting things right is by changing the man seen in the mirror. Though aware of the reality that systems oppress and that other people have a responsibility to set things right, that does not excuse him from his responsibility of trying to set the world right. So he decided that he would begin by looking in the mirror and straightening out the man he sees there:

> If you wanna make the world a better place
> Take a look at yourself, and then make a change.

The place to begin making a difference is by changing the person in the mirror. That may not be all that is necessary but that's the starting place. The place to begin saving a marriage is by changing the person in the mirror. Most of us want to do just the opposite. We want to start remaking our mates. And if a marriage is to be saved, perhaps our mate will have to change also. But while we demand changes of them, it's important that we examine ourselves at the same time. For there are three sides in every situation of conflict—my side, your side, and the truth.

The place to begin making our church into a better church is by changing the person in the mirror. Most of us work just the opposite. When something is amiss we want to change everyone but ourselves. We want to change preachers, musicians, officers, and auxiliary heads. Why seek a new spirit when all we want to do is the same old safe and familiar things with the same old tired and familiar people? The place to begin change is with the person in the mirror so that we can receive a new word from heaven and a fresh anointing of the Holy Spirit.

The person in the mirror is the logical starting point because that individual is really the only person we can change. We cannot make people on the job or in church work right, live right, act right, give right, or do what

> *The person in the mirror is the logical starting point because that individual is really the only person we can change.*

they're supposed to do. The only person's conduct that we have any control over is our own. We can try and try, talk and plead with companions, children, other members of our family and those we love, but we cannot change them. Don't fool yourself. You cannot change anyone other than yourself. More often than not what you see is what you get. You can encourage, assist, and support change. You can pray for change and set an example of change. But change will not take place until the other person is willing to confront the person seen in the mirror and then open up to change. The desire for change may be in us and others, but the power to change does not come from either of us, but from somebody else, whom I'm going to tell you about.

What do we do about the person we see in the mirror? Let's look at how the man in Paul's mirror was redeemed. Paul wrote: "Wretched man that I am! Who will deliver me from this body of death?" What was his answer to this crucial question? It was this: "Thanks be to God through Jesus Christ our Lord!"

As I focused upon the man in my mirror whom I know and love much, like Paul, I was led to another man whom I also know and love much. The man in my mirror is my second greatest asset, the other man is my greatest asset. His name is Jesus. Permit me to tell you something about this Jesus, the man of the cross who helps me deal with the man I see in the mirror, and why I love him so and am so devoted to him. This man understands how I feel as a Black person, because he too was oppressed in the land of his birth. He was a victim of prejudice. When some learned of his background they asked, "Can anything good come out of Nazareth?" He was a rejected man who came unto his own, but his own received him not. However, the rejection of some did not stifle his blessings for others—for as many as received him, to them he gave the power to become the sons and daughters of God.

Jesus was a man's man—all kinds of men were drawn to him. Fiery men like John the Baptist; cursing men like Peter the fisherman; ambitious men like James and John; humble men like Andrew; wise men like Nicodemus; affluent men like a rich young ruler; businessmen like Matthew and Zacchaeus; persecuted men like the ten lepers; men, like blind Bartimaeus, who could not be hushed; determined men like those who uncovered a roof in order to get to him; men, born blind, who could not be bullied; searching men like Nathaniel; cynical men like Thomas; misguided men like Judas; quiet men like James the Lesser and Philip; and men who, like the dying thief on the cross, had committed crimes—were all drawn to him.

Jesus was a woman's man. Women followed him because he was so secure within himself that he never put any of them down to build himself up. Instead he lifted them, loved them without exploiting them, and genuinely respected rather than merely tolerated them. He was a child's man. He said, "Let the children come to me, do not hinder them; for to such belongs the kingdom of God" (Mark 10:14). He was a homeless man. As a babe he was born in a stable, and as an adult, foxes had holes, birds had nests, but he, the Son of man, had no place to lay his head. He was a poor man. When he died, all he owned was the robe on his back. Yet despite his poverty he has made many rich. He was a working man. He was a carpenter by trade and training.

Jesus was a healing man. Ask a man who had lain beside Bethesda's pool for thirty-eight years. Ask a man with a withered hand. Ask a father with an epileptic son. Ask the woman with her issue of blood. Ask a centurion who had a sick servant. Jesus was a man who understood what was in human beings. Ask Legion with his multiple personality disorders. Jesus was a loving man, "Greater love has no man than this, that a man lay down his life for his friends" (John 15:13). He was a man who was not afraid to cry. He wept at the tomb of Lazarus and over the city Jerusalem. He was a praying man, he was known to spend long periods of time talking to his Father in heaven. He was a preaching man whose message was that the kingdom of heaven was at hand. He was a teaching man who could confound the wise and enlighten the simple. He was a singing man. After the Last Supper when he had sung a hymn he went out into the Mount of Olives.

Jesus was a man whose words meant something. The wind and the waves obeyed his command. He was a man of peace. "Tell the daughter of Zion, Behold, your king is coming to you, humble, and mounted on [a donkey]" (Matt. 21:5). He was a man of force. See him with whip in hand as he drove those from the temple who had desecrated God's house. He was a holy man. He was tempted as we are, yet he remained without sin. He was a social man. His enemies accused him of being a friend of sinners. He was a man denied justice. Pilate failed to set him free even though he

> **Jesus was a woman's man. Women followed him because he was so secure within himself that he never put any of them down to build himself up.**

was innocent. He was a man who could hold his temper. He could have called ten thousand angels to destroy this world and set him free. He was a man who could resist a dare. See him as he stayed on the cross when mockers said to him, "If you are the Son of God, I dare you, come down and save yourself."

But above all, he's a triumphant man. That's why he's able to help us: he's victorious. Death couldn't keep him, the grave couldn't hold him. Early that third morning Jesus Christ, my Savior and my Lord, rose with all power to stoop no more. Now he lives and reigns forever.

"Wretched man that I am! Who will deliver me . . . ?
I know a man from Galilee; if you're in trouble, He'll set
   you free.
Oh, do you know Him?"

Chapter Twelve

If God Is for Us, Who Is Against Us?

Romans 8:31

WE HAVE ALL HEARD THE STATEMENT, "If your mind can conceive it and your heart can believe it, then you can achieve it." Like many of you, I affirm and resonate this statement. It speaks to self-empowerment. A major problem with so many of us is that we have no confidence in ourselves. Whenever we're challenged to move into new areas that exceed our zones of comfort, our first response is fear and our first inclination is to say what we cannot do. It is at the point of self-defeatism that we need to hear the statement, "If your mind can conceive it and your heart can believe it, then you can achieve it."

This statement not only speaks to this issue of self-confidence, it also challenges us to have some dreams. Some of us believe that we don't have time to dream. We are caught in such a struggle just to survive from day to day that dreaming is a luxury that we can ill afford either in terms of time or energy. Others of us have been disappointed so often that we are afraid to dream. We feel boxed in by life and our spirits have been broken by so many discouragements that for us, dreaming is a frustrating and futile activity. Still others of us believe that we are so far down that dreaming is useless. We don't doubt our abilities, and our spirits are not broken, but we have just logically looked at our situations and concluded that we can't do any better, and so we have stopped dreaming.

However, the assertion, "if your mind can conceive it and your heart can believe it, then you can achieve it" is a challenge to us to keep dreaming. Never allow anyone or anything, never allow any disappointment, any setback, any foe, any discouraging word, or any mistake to take away your capacity to dream. To dream is to grow, not to dream is to atrophy. To dream is to live, not to dream is to die. Dreams inspire us to reach upward, outward, onward, and inward. Dreams give us a holy discontent. Holy discontent is not anxious restlessness, self-consuming ambition, and greed that never allows us to be either thankful or at peace. Holy discontent inspires and stirs our spirits to keep reaching because God is not finished with us yet. God has something else in this life in store for us.

> *To dream is to grow, not to dream is to atrophy. To dream is to live, not to dream is to die. Dreams inspire us to reach upward, outward, onward, and inward. Dreams give us a holy discontent.*

"If your mind can conceive it and your heart can believe it, then you can achieve it." Every moment of every day, somebody's dream is coming true. Every moment of every day, somebody no smarter than we are, if not as smart; somebody who has as many obstacles as we have, if not more; somebody who has made as many mistakes as we have, if not more; somebody who is just as old as we are, if not older; somebody like us or who doesn't have as much going for him or her as we do has a major dream that is coming true. If their dreams came true, so can ours.

"If your mind can conceive it and your heart can believe it, then you can achieve it." That's a great statement articulating a great truth, yet it is not complete. Life is filled with all kinds of obstacles and stumbling blocks, human influences and demonic forces, and unexpected circumstances such as accidents and sickness. We have no control over these factors that can block a dream. Every life has its share of dream blockers. No matter how much we conceive and believe, we're going to need more than the strength of our own hands to make some things happen. We cannot always drive ourselves by our own steam and expect to reach our goals. We need more than ourselves to achieve some of the dreams of life.

Every worthwhile dream and every great dreamer faces opposition. Whether their names are Joseph or Daniel, Jesus or John, Martin Luther King, Jr. or Fannie Lou Hamer, every worthwhile dream and every great dreamer faces opposition. If our goals are high and lofty, if we are trying to do the right thing, then we will be opposed by evil. No matter how strong we think we are, we can't fight evil by ourselves. Sometimes our thinking can seem so creative or visionary, radical or prophetic, and sometimes it's just different from the norm and goes against the grain, and we will face human opposition of overwhelming odds. We cannot fight overwhelming human opposition ourselves and win.

Anyone with an attitude that says, "it's me against the world," will soon be singing, "it's the world," because the world can crush us. Sometimes people will oppose us out of jealousy and sometimes they will do so out of spite. Some people really do get some sort of cheap thrill out of stepping on and trampling on other folks' dreams. Some people don't want anything worthwhile themselves and resent us for wanting something different. Some people don't have any dreams themselves and resent us for having them. Then there are those who attack dreams either from blindness or ignorance. Everyone doesn't see or understand our dreams and what many of us don't see or understand, we immediately attack. No matter how much we conceive and believe, we're going to need more than ourselves to reach our dreams in the face of overwhelming opposition.

I am aware that the Bible is replete with examples of those who stood against the odds and were victorious. Moses and Aaron opposed one of Egypt's most powerful dynasties and secured the release of God's people from slavery. Joshua and Caleb were justified when they opposed the majority consensus of discouraged freed slaves who wanted to return to Egypt. Samson once slew 1,000 Philistines with the jawbone of an ass. Deborah and the inexperienced Barak defeated the great general Sisera and his mighty army. A shepherd boy named David killed Goliath, a huge giant and seasoned warrior, with only a slingshot. Elijah withstood 450 priests of Baal and 400 prophets of Asherah. Micaiah successfully contradicted the unanimous message of 400 compromised prophets. Daniel's prayer was more powerful than the plot of his enemies and the bite of hungry lions.

Yet none of these persons stood alone. They stood with One who is the true equalizer when the odds are overwhelmingly stacked against us, and who is an advantage giver, no matter how unbalanced the situation. They stood with One whose presence always puts us on the side of the majority. Millennia later, a group of dreamers looked at the odds stacked against them, and then at the One who was for them, and asked a crucial question, "If God is for us, who is against us?" The issue here is not opposition, but victory. We all know that powers, principalities, and people can oppose us. But if God is for us, they will not prevail. I propose that we change our beginning thought from "if your

"If God is for us, who is against us?" The issue here is not opposition, but victory.

mind can conceive it and your heart can believe it, then you can achieve it," to "if your mind can conceive it and your heart can believe it, then with God, you can achieve it."

Thus, my message is a very simple one: Keep your dreams no matter how far-fetched, unreachable, or impossible they may seem. For, "if God is for us, who is against us?" We're going to encounter disappointments and setbacks along the way. No one ever reached a goal without experiencing some setbacks. Setbacks are part of progress, even as mistakes are part of learning. Some setbacks can be so devastating and discouraging that we truly feel like giving up and our dreams seem lost forever. However, when we encounter such setbacks there is a crucial question that we need to ask ourselves, "If God is for us, who is against us?"

Keep your dreams no matter what opposition you encounter or who fails to actively support you. One of the most discouraging moments in the life of a dreamer occurs when she or he discovers that some of those who were listed in the asset column are found in the liability column. In other words, some people we had counted on being with us are either actively fighting us or failing to support us. Sometimes people don't do anything to hurt us, but they don't do anything to help us either. They feel that their refusal to help is not hurting us. However, dead weight is not easier to carry because it isn't kicking. Dead weight is still a burden. Those who fail to support us can be just as discouraging as those who fight against us. However when those whom we thought were assets turn out to be liabilities, let us remember our truest and greatest asset and ask ourselves a crucial question for discouraging moments, "If God is for us, who is against us?"

However, dead weight is not easier to carry because it isn't kicking. Dead weight is still a burden.

Keep your dreams no matter how weak you may feel at any given moment. Show me a person who has never been discouraged, and I'll show you a person who has never tried to do anything or become anything worthwhile. Show me a person who has never doubted and I'll show you a person who has never really believed. Show me a person who has never been afraid and I'll show you a person who has never undertaken a challenge. Even the most positive among us feels negative sometimes; even the most cheerful among us gets depressed sometimes; even the most determined among us feels like giving up sometimes. Everybody has an Achilles' heel in the spirit where Satan can reach and discouragement can touch. However, when we reach those points in our lives, there is a crucial question we need to ask ourselves, "If God is for us, who is against us?"

There is a fascinating book called *I Dream a World* that is filled with biographical sketches of a few twentieth-century Black women of distinction. When we consider the past and present living hells to which Black women have been subjected, some may conclude that for them to dream of a career, or of true romantic love, or of a liberated gender or race would be sufficient. However, for the maligned and powerless daughters of Africa to dream a world would seem unthinkable. Where do Black women get the tenacity to dream a world? They have discovered the answer to a very crucial question, "If God is for us, who is against us?"

Martin Luther King, Jr. dreamed of a nation in which his children would not be judged by the color of their skin but

Where do Black women get the tenacity to dream a world? They have discovered the answer to a very crucial question, "If God is for us, who is against us?"

by the content of their character. He dreamed a world in which nations would beat their swords into plowshares and their spears into pruning hooks and would study war no more. How could this battered and misunderstood prophet have such a dream that still speaks to the deep yearnings of our spirits and souls? King discovered the answer to a very crucial question, "If God is for us, who is against us?"

How do some of us know that we can kick the habits that have kicked us in the past? How do we know that we can live free from drink and drugs and other things? How do we know that there is life after our mistakes and failures? How do we know that we can rise from disgrace to dignity? Some of us have found the answer to a crucial question, "If God is for us, who is against us?"

"If your mind can conceive it and your heart can believe it, then with God you can achieve it." And we know that in all things God works for the good of those who love him, who have been called according to his purpose. "What then shall we say to this? If God is for us, who is against us? He who did not spare his own Son but gave him up for us all, will he not also give us all things with him? Who shall bring any charge against God's elect? It is God who justifies; who is to condemn? Is it Christ Jesus, who died, yes, who was raised from the dead, who is at the right hand of God, who indeed intercedes for us? Who shall separate us from the love of Christ? Shall tribulation, or distress, or persecution, or famine, or nakedness, or peril, or sword? As it is written, 'For thy sake we are being killed all the day long; we are regarded as sheep to be slaughtered.' No, in all these things we are more than conquerors through him who loved us. For I am sure that neither death, nor life, nor angels, nor principalities, nor things present, nor things to come, nor powers, nor height, nor depth, nor anything else in all creation, will be able to separate us from the love of God in Christ Jesus our Lord" (Rom. 8:31-39).